# A MILLION MILES FOR CELTIC

# A MILLION MILES FOR CELTIC

An Autobiography

## Bobby Lennox, MBE
with Gerry McNee

Foreword by Jock Stein, CBE

### Stanley Paul
London Melbourne Sydney Auckland Johannesburg

To Kathryn and Rosaleen ...
also Gillian, Gary, Jeffrey, and Dara,
Kathleen and Little Rosaleen

Stanley Paul & Co. Ltd

An imprint of the Hutchinson Publishing Group

17–21 Conway Street, London W1P 6JD

Hutchinson Group (Australia) Pty Ltd
30–32 Cremorne Street, Richmond South, Victoria 3121
PO Box 151, Broadway, New South Wales 2007

Hutchinson Group (NZ) Ltd
32–34 View Road, PO Box 40-086, Glenfield, Auckland 10

Hutchinson Group (SA) Pty Ltd
PO Box 337, Bergvlei 2012, South Africa

First published 1982

Set in Baskerville by Computape (Pickering) Ltd,
Pickering, North Yorkshire

Printed in Great Britain by The Anchor Press Ltd
and bound by Wm Brendon & Son Ltd,
both of Tiptree, Essex

ISBN 0 09 150240 3

The authors would like to express their gratitude
to Mr Pat Woods for certain statistical
materials

# Contents

# Foreword
### By JOCK STEIN, CBE

I could write my own book about Bobby Lennox because there are so many good things to say about him. He was the kind of player who epitomized what every manager looks for in a professional. He looked after himself, knowing that there would be plenty of time to enjoy an easier life when his playing days were over.

Many players come to the big city, sign for the big clubs and then think they are big shots. But Bobby decided against city life and instead stayed close to his roots in his native Saltcoats. After training at Parkhead in the morning, he would build up his tremendous pace even further by running along the sands opposite his home in the afternoons. At the same time he remained the uncomplicated person he had always been: he stuck by the ways he knew best.

In a playing sense he was exceptional but in a different way from those around him. He was possibly one of the lesser-known names in our great side of the sixties and I say this with the greatest of respect for him because the Johnstones, Aulds, Murdochs and Gemmells grabbed the headlines. Yet most of their play would have come to nothing unless Bobby had been at the end of it.

The fact that he got less publicity meant that he got away with a lot more at times on the field because some people foolishly did not give him the respect he deserved. Not everyone appreciated his ability to read the game better than many an opponent. They soon learned though when he punished them the best way he could – by putting the ball in the net, the ultimate answer in football. His ability to get into scoring positions was uncanny and his fantastic pace often saw him pulled up for being offside in marginal situations.

Despite having more reason than most to get upset about decisions, he was sporting both on and off the field. He just wanted to play football as it should be played and he loved scoring goals. If a ball came back off a post or the crossbar he was there to put it away. And he chased balls others wouldn't dream could be caught, often turning the impossible into a winning goal for Celtic.

Perhaps one of the best tributes paid to him was from Bobby Charlton, a man who graced the highest levels of the game. After he played alongside Bobby in a testimonial match Charlton said his own career could have been extended three to five years had Lennox been by his side.

When I arrived back at Parkhead in 1965 there had been talk of Bobby going to Falkirk, but even then I was aware of his great pace and felt he had a lot to offer. I soon discovered that his fitness was quite incredible. He was the one player who never needed pre-season training because he never allowed himself to be in anything but top condition. He was about five weeks ahead of everyone else in terms of fitness at the start of each season. He always wanted to play and was seldom unavailable.

It was the American tour of 1966 which was his making. We developed the midfield of Murdoch and Auld with Johnstone lying deep to distract and pull people away from the area Lennox could exploit with his pace. He developed a tremendous understanding with Auld and revelled in the service of passing from the midfield. You could always depend on him to come up trumps and score on the crunch occasions.

Perhaps the finest tribute I can pay him is to say that he was all that's good in the game and a great clubman. He played at the highest level for twenty years yet left without having an enemy on or off the field.

# Introduction

By GERRY McNEE

Chief Sports Writer, *Scottish Daily Express*


Bobby Lennox, Member of the British Empire, last of the Lisbon Lions, record postwar goalscorer, record medal winner ... a darting, flying forward whose searing speed burned the spirit out of defenders.

Every superlative in the book was used to eulogize the man whose playing career spanned the best part of two decades and coincided with Celtic's zenith.

Career, in fact, is an inadequate term in the case of Lennox, who played at the highest level for so long. The word 'history' has a more appropriate ring to it.

The 'Buzz-bomb', the 'Electric hare' or just plain 'Lemon' as he's known at Celtic Park won a record eleven championship medals and a record eight Scottish Cup awards between 1965 and his retirement towards the end of 1980.

He also played in two European Champions' Cup finals in Lisbon (1967) and Milan (1970).

Today he is coach to Celtic's successful reserve team, still channelling his unbounded enthusiasm into the club he loves above all others. The sheer respect he commands from the young players is self-explanatory. They simply hold the man and his achievements in awe. They appreciate that he was a member of a team which strode so impressively across the world stage that no side could feel safe against them. The European aristocrats such as Real Madrid, Inter Milan, Liverpool, Leeds and the rest treated them as at least dangerous equals.

Lennox was essentially a speed player – an attribute

9

which once moved Jock Stein, his manager for so long, to comment that the player's goal tally would have been much greater had linesmen been able to come to terms with his reflexes and speed over the first few vital yards.

His magnificent attitude to training together with his self-discipline were two ingredients which made him the exception rather than the rule in his playing days. The men who have enjoyed longevity in football have been the sweepers and the midfield generals, who use their experience to compensate for ageing legs and lungs.

The survival of Lennox at the highest level depended on his pace; his effectiveness had always been inseparable from quickness. In his prime he was without doubt one of the genuine runners in world football. At the age of thirty-seven, when forced by a bad muscular injury to retire from the playing side, he was still one of the fastest men in football.

Another vital ingredient of the Lennox make-up was his insatiable appetite for playing. As you will read in the pages ahead, this conquered all. He was a man who just wanted a ball at his feet, pressures and problems were not a part of his life. To him fitness and training were as much psychological as physical.

There's one particular story about Lennox which probably sums up his philosophy of age and fitness. At the age of thirty-three his leg was broken in a match against Rangers at Ibrox, yet his reaction to an injury which should have slammed the door shut on even the bravest footballer's career, was characteristic. 'I actually believe,' he said at the time, 'that having my leg in plaster did me a lot of good. I've always been plagued by ankle injuries – especially to the right ankle. Probably when you're a bit on the quick side, defenders – even when not trying to foul – tend to nick you there as you go past, and that type of damage never really gets the proper time to heal.

'Maybe the manager is hustling you to get back for an important match, or you're itching to get back yourself. The one thing about having a leg in plaster is that everyone's sorry for you and you know yourself that time is required. So by the time I made my comeback my ankles were sound. That injury might have done me a good turn.'

Any footballer who can make a blessing out of breaking a leg at thirty-three years of age has to be special!

A couple of years later he was freed by Jock Stein, but after just a few months playing in American soccer he was re-signed by new manager Billy McNeill who was short of players with the spirit and commitment required by Celtic.

McNeill's move was to lead to an Indian summer of glory which included a championship win of dramatic proportions with a vital Lennox goal keeping the challenge alive in a match against St Mirren at Ibrox.

Then, in a Scottish Cup tie – again against St Mirren – he was to play ninety minutes plus half-an-hour of extra time in a Celtic team reduced to ten men. He had scored a penalty ten minutes from time to send the match to that period of extra time and Celtic went on to win. He walked from the Love Street pitch as fresh as team-mates and opponents half his age.

And in keeping with the fairy-tale fashion of his era he appeared in the final against Rangers at Hampden to collect that record eighth winners' medal.

His conduct on and off the field saw him emerge as the greatest example of his generation to youngsters hoping to make a career in football.

It was fitting indeed that Celtic found a place for him when injury finished his incredible career.

# 1

# The Reluctant Footballer

When I look back over the past couple of decades and all the great moments and successes I've shared with the greatest club in the world I still have to pinch myself to make sure it's all true. You see, there was a time when Bobby Lennox just couldn't bring himself to play in organized football.

I walked out on my primary school team never having played a single game for them and I had to be literally forced to turn out at secondary level. Even when Celtic came for me I almost made a mess of things and the build-up to my first-team debut was, to say the least, a comedy of errors.

It's only in recent years that I've come fully to appreciate what was wrong in those early days. Anyone who knows me now is aware that I'm a happy-go-lucky type, but I was a shy wee boy then and the thought of having to prove my ability in football to older boys – especially strangers – shattered me.

From a fairly early age it became apparent that I wasn't bad at the game. Ours was a footballing family, with my two older brothers Andrew and Eric involved at junior and Scottish schoolboys' level. My teachers seemed to think I had what was required so every afternoon I headed straight home and then out to practise with the ball. But never once did I say I wanted to be a professional footballer or even thought I might be good enough. It was just something that was to happen quite naturally over many years.

Apart from being a footballing home it was also a happy home. My father was a bookmaker and my mother a lady barber – the only one in Saltcoats. Almost from the time I was able to walk I kicked a ball in the streets of that same Saltcoats on the Ayrshire coast – where I still live today with my own wife and children.

Hitler was at our throats when I was born on 30 August 1943 at number 2 Quay Street, a little two-storey tenement just a hundred yards from the harbour.

Amongst my earliest childhood memories is that of falling into the harbour and getting a hiding when I got home. At the age of four we moved up the high road away from the temptations of the water, but not before I had committed another indiscretion which I can laugh at now but which mortified me at that early and tender age. Being wartime everything was in short supply but my father had managed to get some black-market sugar which he brought home in a large biscuit tin. One cold evening nature called Bobby Lennox, but he didn't fancy making the trip to the outside toilet. And little boys being little boys he, for reasons best known to himself, decided to pee into the biscuit tin. He was totally fascinated to see the contents of the box change colour! I've told that little tale in the third person because it's still painful to remember the aftermath!

I was about eight years of age when I was first chosen to play for St Mary's Primary School Under-12s and that was when I first began to show a reluctance to play in organized matches.

Our jerseys – blue with white sleeves – were handed to us at lunchtime and I was told that some of the older lads would call at the classroom for me at 3.30 when the bus arrived. The fact that even today I live only two hundred yards from where I was born shows what a home bird I really am. And in those days the thought of going to Ardrossan – just a couple of miles away – seemed like the ends of the earth. As the afternoon wore on I got more and more nervous and I remember sitting in the classroom looking at my Hopalong Cassidy watch ... 3.20 ... 3.25

... 3.30 ... 3.40.... By this time my stomach was in a knot, worse than it could ever be years later before a match played in front of 100,000 people.

Whether the bus still hadn't arrived or whether the older boys had forgotten to call for me I can't remember now. But by this time the waiting had become too much and I handed the jersey back to the teacher saying, 'I'm not playing'. I picked up my schoolbag and headed home.

Despite that the teachers continued to pick me for the team, game after game. They told me I was the best player in the school and even banned me from playground kick abouts so that I would be fit for the school team.

But no matter how much I was coaxed I never played for the primary and it was to be the same, at first, when I moved on to St Michael's. Someone there told the teachers I should be in the team and they made attempts to get me to play – without success.

Then one morning, quite by accident, I broke down part of that particular barrier. On Saturdays I always went down to the playing fields to watch a game but I always timed it so that I arrived late and I couldn't be asked to take part. A local team called St John's were playing the Scouts and the kickoff had been delayed because the Scouts were a man short. Before I could refuse I found myself lining up at left-half and I made a scoring debut when I rifled the ball into the back of my own net! But I hit two into the correct goal in the second half which got me an invitation to play for St John's the following week and I accepted. That match brought the break-through at school too, and I began enjoying my football.

On Saturday mornings I had a milk run – and when I say run I mean run. I had two great pals who are still friends today – Tommy Burns and Joseph Murray – and they can take some of the credit for my career. Tommy and I developed great lungs running alongside the milk cart and I'm sure that's where I got my speed. At the end of the run, beside the football parks, was Joseph's house and his mother used to have a good meal ready for me so that I could go straight to my game. And while I was playing Tommy would get a lift on the cart, collect my bike and bring it to the pitches so I would have transport home.

My play was certainly attracting attention because the next thing to happen to me was my being chosen for the Ayrshire trials (which were being held in Irvine). I left school one afternoon with two friends who had also been chosen, everything was fine and I remember the nuns from the school shouting, 'Good luck Bobby'. But within an hour everything had gone wrong for me again. When we arrived I heard one of the teachers say, 'Right, let's get two teams organized here,' and he joked, 'We'll call it the probables against the possibles.' Suddenly I found I was on the opposite side from my two pals and the old knot returned to the stomach despite the fact that I was by then fourteen years old. I was surrounded by strange faces and I told the teacher I couldn't play.

I remember him saying, 'Look Bobby, this isn't a trial for you, you're in the Ayrshire team and if you do well here you'll end up playing for Scotland.' But not even that could boost my confidence and I picked up my schoolbag and left. Next day the teachers were furious with me and they went to see my mother. Very soon young Bobby was playing again!

From school I went on to play for the Star of the Sea team where my brothers had played. In my younger days I had accompanied Eric and Andrew and enjoyed banging the ball into the nets after I had helped put them up. Now I was doing it in earnest and it wasn't long before Ardeer Recreation came for me. By this stage I had turned fifteen.

I had eighteen happy months there and well remember my debut against Saltcoats Vics at Recreation Park – the finest junior ground in the country. We were leading 3–0 at half-time thanks to a hat trick by new-boy Lennox only for the full-time score to read 4–3 for Vics.

It was during my spell at Ardeer that Celtic arrived on the scene. Falkirk, Motherwell and Kilmarnock were interested. And English clubs such as Chelsea and

Blackpool were also showing interest. Chelsea invited me south and I cried for three days in London. It was obvious to them that I couldn't stay there and they gave me my fare home. Even Falkirk seemed a million miles away and no one – including my family – knew just how much of a home bird I was. My pals would say, 'You're waiting for Celtic to come along'.

Yet in those days I wasn't a great Celtic supporter although we were a Celtic family and went to see them occasionally. But my dad would rather give me and my pals money to go over to Rugby Park or Clyde and Queen's Park to keep us away from the big crowds. Yet the night we went up to Celtic Park to see manager Jimmy McGrory about my signing on, I could see my father was really proud and thrilled as Mr McGrory showed us around the place.

Other clubs had offered to call me up right away, while Celtic's offer that night was simply to sign a provisional form. But I didn't have to be asked twice and I signed on the dotted line. It wasn't till that moment that I realized just how much the name Celtic meant to me. My pals must have been right because even the thought of the travel to a big place like Glasgow didn't enter my head. There was obviously only one club in the world for Bobby Lennox and that club was Glasgow Celtic.

Their approach had come after a game against Shettleston in the West of Scotland Cup. They were a right good team in those days and had beaten us 4–1 at home, although I had the consolation of getting Ardeer's goal. As I walked off the park feeling a bit sorry for myself the manager told me the Celtic scout wanted a chat. Their chief scout was Joe Connors whom I'd seen a couple of times before. Sadly, Joe has since died but I'll always remember his opening remark to me that day, 'I'll put it on the line to you, Bobby, how would you like to put your future in the hands of the Glasgow Celtic?' Before I could reply he added, 'Report to Celtic Park with your dad at six o'clock on Tuesday night'.

After signing me, Mr McGrory told me that since I

lived out of town I need only report once a week for training, but once more I almost made a mess of things through my shyness.

Six weeks later I got a letter from Celtic asking what had happened to me and would I please report for training. Yes, I'd failed to turn up again. I had been training away with Ardeer knowing full well I should have been travelling to Parkhead. I knew Celtic were expecting me but I felt I should wait for some official word.

So I set off for Parkhead by train on Tuesday, arriving at Central Station at about half-past-four and with time to spare. I wandered about the town centre wondering whether I'd make it as a player at this level. At that stage life was happy enough but far from perfect. I worked at ICI in a box factory and it was a dire job. I really hated it and the best moment of the day came when I heard the hooter go. There had to be more to life, I remember thinking.

I walked along to Glasgow Cross and, not knowing which tram to take, I got into a taxi and again shyness got a hold of me. I told the driver to take me out to the London Road and that I was going to an address near Celtic Park. I was afraid to tell him to take me right up to the front door in case he thought I was some sort of bighead.

As we approached I recognized the place because of the huge black bridge across the main road and I told him to let me out there. I walked through the front door of Celtic Park at exactly six o'clock feeling quite happy with my timekeeping, but the place was very quiet – not a soul about.

Then a door opened and Sean Fallon, the assistant manager, appeared speaking in that unmistakable Irish brogue which seemed to get stronger with each passing year in Scotland, 'What d'ya want, son?'

I was shaking with nerves and said almost in a whisper, 'I was told to report for training.'

'Who told you to report for training?'

'Mr McGrory wrote me a letter and asked me to report,' I replied.

18

'What's your name then?' asked Sean.

I told him and a warm smile appeared, 'Oh,' he said, 'Robert. We've been waiting patiently for you, come on in.'

I had never met Sean or anyone else at Celtic Park apart from the scout and Mr McGrory – I really was a stranger in Paradise – because I had signed without so much as playing a trial.

As Sean walked me to the dressing room to get kitted out all the players were already on the park. The letter had said that training was at 6 p.m. sharp – I had read it as arriving at six. When I think back to that particular episode I sometimes wonder how I managed a twenty-year playing career with the club and still find myself in the same surroundings today!

The first contact I made with the players was while lapping the track or between exercises. There were players like Bobby Murdoch, Tommy Gemmell, Willie O'Neill and Jimmy Johnstone who was on the staff as a ball boy. I was made to feel quite at home and it wasn't to be too long before I got my first break.

The Barrowfield training ground had a red ash pitch which was used by the third team for their matches and I got word to report there on the Saturday morning. To be honest I was worried about playing on ash. Then came my lucky break with a phone call to the factory telling me to forget Saturday. I was to report to Celtic Park on Friday night to play for the Reserves against Falkirk. A lad at the factory offered to give me a lift up to Glasgow, I made my debut on Celtic Park itself and played well in a 2–0 win. I looked on that as one of the big breaks of my career because I felt I would let myself down playing on a surface which was foreign to me.

A short time later Ardeer were knocked out of the Scottish Cup and Celtic called me up to a steady place in the Reserves. But the Lennox career, it seemed, was in a big hurry and another break saw me get the chance to play in the first team after only four appearances with the second eleven and four goals in those matches.

When I got out of bed on the morning of Saturday, 3 March 1962 little did I know what was in store for me. We were due to meet Dundee Reserves at Dens Park and I went to Ferrari's Restaurant in Glasgow – the Celtic meeting place in those days – to await the team bus. When it appeared Sean Fallon stepped off and told me, 'You've not to travel Bobby. Steve Chalmers has flu and Mike Jackson is injured and you could be playing in the first team.' The other young players came pouring off the bus to congratulate me as I almost collapsed with shock. I was totally stunned. I thought someone like Bobby Murdoch would get the chance first so I really appreciated him and the other lads wishing me well.

The weather was still wintry and I needed rubber boots so Sean scribbled out a credit line for the Sportsman's Emporium and I set off running down Renfield Street. I picked up the boots and began running towards Argyle Street and then along to Glasgow Cross. I was in a blind panic but I remember stopping to phone my pal Joseph Murray. We had no phone at home and I wanted him to let my dad know that I was likely to be in the first team. Suddenly my mind began to clear a bit. What was I doing at Glasgow Cross? Obviously I had set out to run to Celtic Park. But then I remembered Sean's instructions. I was supposed to go back to Ferrari's.

So again I sprinted through the city centre streets with my new boots under my arm and I got back to the restaurant in time for a light lunch. Frank Haffey, Paddy Crerand and Jim Kennedy were all awaiting me there and must have wondered who the sweaty wee fellow was. They helped settle me down before calling a taxi.

I remember travelling through the huge crowds as we approached the ground with the fans waving to the three established players. The atmosphere was fantastic because Dundee were the opposition and were going for the championship, which they were to win eventually despite the fact that we beat them 2–1 that day in front of a crowd of 39,000.

We headed into the dressing room, and I met the rest of

the team for the very first time at ten-past-two. One asked me, 'Are you in the first team, son?' That didn't do my confidence much good but luckily time was so short that the next thing I remember is jogging out onto the park. It wasn't a great game for me and early in the second half I had the unusual experience of going down with cramp. What I knew, though no one else did, was that it was all due to nervous tension. Paddy Crerand picked me up and shouted, 'Get forward Bobby, forward.' Then after thirty-three minutes I thought a dream had come true when I had the ball in the net only to have the goal disallowed for no real reason. In fact I felt I had been fouled by Dundee centre-half Ian Ure as I got past him to hit the ball. Apparently it was alleged I'd handled the ball but I know I didn't – and Cyril Horne in the *Glasgow Herald* stated, 'I did not detect that infringement.'

But Cyril wasn't exactly overflowing with praise when he added: 'Lennox found the pace of his first Scottish League game overwhelming and none of his forward colleagues were capable of coaxing him into confidence.' Little did he know that I had done an impromptu training session through the centre of Glasgow in the hours leading up to the game!

'Waverley', the *Daily Record* correspondent, was a bit more kind: 'The month-old senior Lennox tried hard and revealed quite a good soccer brain.' And in the *Sunday Mail* their columnist said: 'The Celtic front line, with the obviously clever but so very immature Lennox having little impact, were continually baulked by the Dundee defence.' Anyway, some of the fans were pleased with the result, as a few ran onto the field at the end to give some back-slaps to the Celtic players.

The teams that day were: Celtic – Haffey, McKay, Kennedy; Crerand, McNeill, Price; F. Brogan, Lennox, Hughes, Divers, Carroll. Dundee – Liney, Hamilton, Cox; Seith, Ure, Brown; Smith, Cousin, Wishart, Gilzean, Robertson.

Brogan and McNeill got our goals with Wishart having opened the scoring fifteen minutes into the second half.

Frank and then Billy with the winner both struck in the final ten minutes to give me at least a winning start.

By the following week Steve Chalmers and Mike Jackson were fit, and I promptly returned to the Reserves – although it wasn't to be too long until yet another chance came along.

Celtic arranged a friendly match against Johnstone Burgh and it was used as a comeback match for Big John Hughes who had been injured. I played alongside him and it paid off, with me getting a hat trick and the team leading 4–1 at half-time. Afterwards, to my astonishment, Mr McGrory told me to report to Hampden the following night. My heart missed a beat or two because Celtic were due to play Third Lanark in the Glasgow Cup final and I had only one first team game behind me.

As it turned out I was a spectator in the stand but the match finished in a 1–1 draw and I got my chance in the replay at Celtic Park, no doubt thanks to those goals against Johnstone Burgh. We lost Billy McNeill through injury that night in pouring wet conditions but with ten men went on to record a fine 3–2 victory against an all-star team which, among others, boasted Hilley, Gray and Harley. So, after only two first team appearances I was the proud owner of a winners' medal – one I treasure to this day. It was only the second trophy Celtic had won since the famous 7–1 League Cup victory over Rangers in 1957 (Celtic had also won the Glasgow Charity Cup in 1959) and we got a fabulous reception from the fans.

The Glasgow Cup at that time was a very successful and highly thought of competition; unlike today when it has to take a back seat to other championships. Little did anyone realize that night that the victory was to be merely an oasis in a desert of non-success and that several more years in the wilderness were to follow.

For me it wasn't a bad thing to go back to the Reserves where I served a good apprenticeship with many of the players who were to go on to Lisbon glory and win so many medals – players like Fallon, Young, Gemmell, Cushley, Clark, Johnstone, Murdoch and Gallagher. We certainly managed to dominate that Reserve league in those years. I missed much of the very good run in the European Cup Winners' Cup in 1963–4, making only six first team appearances. But there was one milestone – my first goal for the first team in a league match against Third Lanark on 14 September 1963. Just to ruin the occasion we managed only a 4–4 draw after leading 4–0!

The *Sunday Mail* described my goal thus, 'Joe Davis, the Thirds full back, badly mistimed his pass-back to keeper Stewart Mitchell and before either quite knew what had happened, the flying Lennox had pounced and stabbed the ball into the net.'

There was a rather flattering article in the *Daily Record* a few days before that game which praised my partnership with Paddy Turner in a game against Rangers. 'Paddy can thank his right-wing partner, quiet man Bobby Lennox, because bustling Bobby took a great deal of the weight off him. Lennox brings a touch of the unorthodox to the right-wing business. He is not a winger in the traditional Celtic mould. He doesn't have the Delaney dash, the Collins craft, the Bertie Thomson footwork – but the former Ardeer Rec. junior played a highly serviceable match against Rangers.

'At Ibrox Bobby baffled Jim Baxter and Davie Provan – not by dazzle stuff on the ball, but by the power of his tackling with the tremendous strength of his short, stocky legs. Time and again he won the ball and time and again survived rough tackles.'

The article – my first major write-up – advised Celtic to keep me on the right wing and went on to quote chairman Bob Kelly as stating that I could become a Celtic 'great'.

Despite that type of praise I was determined to keep my feet on the ground. I made my European debut the following week in the Cup Winners' Cup against Basle and scored my second first-team goal in a fine 5–1 victory.

Our line-up on 17 September 1963 was: Haffey, McKay, Gemmell; McNamee, McNeill, Clark; Lennox, Chalmers, Hughes, Divers, F. Brogan. As I said, I missed most of the good European run which saw our young side surprise everyone and reach the semifinals only to lose 4–3 on aggregate to Hungarians M.T.K. Budapest. This was without doubt the first sign that the club's youth policy was bearing fruit.

I scored just two goals in my six appearances but the following season – 1964–5 – I broke back into the team and started enjoying a run of goals. I remember it all beginning in a match against Morton at Cappielow where we were three up and almost lost it 4–3 in the dying minutes only for Morton to have a goal disallowed.

We started a good Scottish Cup run in January 1965 and I scored in every round leading up to the final, including a semifinal replay against Motherwell at Hampden. But before those semifinals were to be played, something momentous was to happen to the Celtic Football Club. In one of the most significant happenings in its history a man named Jock Stein was appointed manager.

I had read about him and heard about him but when I saw the headlines in the newspapers my first thought was, Oh no, here I am doing quite well and now I could be out on my neck. As it turned out my fears were unfounded. He kept me in the team, we won the Scottish Cup and little did I know at that stage just what a profound effect this new manager was to have on the career of Bobby Lennox.

# 2

# The Stein Revolution

When it came to team selections Jock Stein was the most ruthless man in the world. Yet as far as Glasgow Celtic were concerned the ends justified the means, as his methods brought unparalleled success while at the same time ensuring that the players had a real hunger for the jersey. It's an understatement to say that he ruled with a fist of iron and that we were all in awe of him. We would report to Parkhead on match days and wait in the dressing room till he appeared and, believe me, no matter who you happened to be, no matter how well you had played in recent games, there was no guarantee you would play that day. It had such an effect that when you heard your name on the team-sheet you couldn't get the jersey over your head quick enough to get out there and prove yourself all over again.

My biggest lesson in that department came just before we won the European Cup in 1967 and at that time I had been a regular. It's got to be every player's ambition to play at Wembley – especially against England. At the start of the week I had been named in the national squad and I was over the moon. As we prepared at Seamill to play Dukla Prague in the semifinals of the Champions' Cup it was Jock Stein who brought me the news I would play at Wembley – and then told me I was dropped for the Dukla game! I was good enough to play against the World Champions that week (and I scored) yet not good enough for my club. But you accepted these things from Jock because there was always a good reason.

On another occasion in Europe I was confiding in my wee pal Jimmy Johnstone that I reckoned I was for the chop after a bad game. Jimmy and I always shared a room, and I remember a couple of hours before the match the manager popped his head round the door and told me I was playing but that Jimmy was dropped. You could have knocked over the Wee Man with a feather.

There was a lighter side to it all as well. The previous year I recall the trip to Bermuda and America – a reward from the club for winning the championship. A few days before we left we were in the dressing room after training; even at this late stage no one knew for certain whether or not they were going to be in the squad. Big Jock suddenly appeared with the passports and visas and began handing them out.

'Here you are Tam, Bobby, Bertie ...' One man on tenterhooks was Willie O'Neill, a fine fullback who had lost his place in the team but was still very much a part of the squad. The manager handed him a folder and as he turned away Willie couldn't hide his delight as he threw a clenched fist heavenwards. Quick as a flash Jock spun round and said, 'Willie, did I give you one of these?'

'Yes boss,' replied Willie.

'Sorry,' said the Big Man, 'I've made a mistake.' As he went to take it back Willie turned white until he saw the impish grin spread over the Stein face.

Joke though it was, it summed up for me the absolute power of the man over his players; it made you desperate to play for him.

The fact that most of us were young and single at the time meant that we could travel at the drop of a hat without facing domestic pressures but, more than ten years later when the club embarked on its farthest-ever tour to the Far East, players were again kept waiting till the last minute. With just about everybody married with children there were domestic pressures this time, and you'll remember that Kenny Dalglish pulled out of that tour having just returned with Scotland from an exhausting trip to South America.

But that was Jock Stein, who arrived on the scene in early 1965 to revolutionize the club. One newspaper headline screamed: 'First-ever Protestant boss of Celtic'. But I never found that religion was taken into account at Parkhead. As players we were simply apprehensive about a man arriving with the reputation he had – a reputation for transforming ailing clubs into winners.

On a personal note, the 1964–5 season had seen me become almost a regular at outside left making a total of thirty-seven appearances in the league, League Cup, Scottish Cup and Glasgow Cup. We had reached the final of the League Cup for the first time in seven years with a blistering run in the qualifying section. After a disappointing 0–0 home draw against Partick Thistle we beat Hearts 3–0 at Tynecastle and 6–1 at Parkhead. We scored five against Thistle at Firhill and had a convincing 4–1 victory over Kilmarnock to reach the quarterfinals where we beat East Fife 6–2 on aggregate. I didn't play in all of these games but I did play a crucial part in the semifinal against Morton.

On 29 September 1964 we lined up against the Cappielow club at Ibrox in front of 55,000 spectators and I got one of the goals in a 2–0 victory. But as luck would have it I didn't get a place in the final, which Rangers won 2–1 amidst some controversy when Jimmy Johnstone appeared to have scored only for the referee to judge that the ball hadn't crossed the line. Celtic got few breaks in those days!

However the press were beginning to take notice of us and one report described us as 'the best Celtic side in years'. It went on to state: 'Prominent in the side is Bobby Lennox, a goal maker, if not a goal taker whose accurate passing and crossing, allied to his pace, are making chances for his colleagues.' Not a bad reference I'd say!

In January 1965 Bertie Auld had returned to the club after his exile at Birmingham and you could sense straight away the professionalism he had acquired in the south where he had sampled European football at a very high level. Bertie was an instant hit with the younger players. He gave us confidence and was a great man for settling the nerves with a joke. He always had a cracker up his sleeve for match days in the dressing room and it was always eagerly awaited.

So with all of this going for us it was only natural that the morning papers of 1 February gave us a bit of a jolt. The previous afternoon, unknown to the players, chairman Bob Kelly had called a press conference and announced that Jock Stein was taking over the following month. Although championship performances were dreadful we kept winning in the Scottish Cup, beating St Mirren, Queen's Park and Kilmarnock to reach the semifinals: it was just a couple of days after beating Killie that Stein arrived at Parkhead. Everything was in a whirl at the ground as we waited to meet him for the first time, and I vividly remember his walking into the dressing room. He had such presence that as soon as he started speaking you could have heard a pin drop, he commanded a respect I'd never witnessed before.

Some of the lads already knew him from his coaching days at Parkhead before he had left for Dunfermline. The likes of Bertie Auld, John Clark and Billy McNeill had worked under him but he had grown in stature and reputation since those times.

The most immediate changes came in training when he introduced us to set-pieces. I remember the first thing he had us working at alarmed me. Suddenly I thought football was going to become just too complicated for me. But it didn't take him long to convince you that it could be done with a bit of hard work.

Practically every part of training was done with the ball and everyone was handed one on the way onto the park. Before Stein we had been used to lapping the track. But this way you'd get through a good bit of work without really feeling the effects. I always had the theory that training is a state of mind and this proved it beyond all doubt. We'd jog with the ball and sprint with it and enjoy it.

Before Stein we would train for two hours and no matter how much work you had got through, those in charge of the training would keep you lapping the track while keeping an eye on the watch. It had to be two hours exactly and boy, did we feel it!

Stein was a great one for saying, 'Right lads, let's get in a good half hour's work.' He showed us that we could achieve as much in that time – and probably more – than we had done in the past. We learned that football is all about recovery – getting in a quick sprint and doubling back.

This was the kind of lesson that was to come back to me on my first day in charge of the reserve side towards the end of 1980. We were playing the first team and John Halpin was facing Danny McGrain. I was telling him to forget about Danny's reputation and experience and use his pace to take him on. At one stage Danny got in a good tackle and set off with the ball into our penalty area while John casually jogged back. The goalkeeper got the ball and threw it back out to John who immediately found himself being tackled again by Danny who hadn't stopped running.

'That,' I said, in my first lecture as a coach, 'is how to play the game.' Danny had kept going in the knowledge that he'd get a rest when the ball went to the other side of the park. But while it was in his territory there was no let-up. John had been taking a break at the wrong time which was a very common fault among players at Parkhead before Stein arrived and taught us the importance of recovery.

We were all obviously out to impress him in his first game in charge, which was a league match in midweek against Airdrie at Broomfield Park. We played out of our skins and won 6–0 with Bertie Auld getting no fewer than five of the goals.

It was Bertie who kept us in the Scottish Cup with a penalty equalizer against Motherwell in the semifinals at Hampden after a centre-forward called Joe McBride had given his side a 2–1 lead. We convincingly won the replay the following Wednesday by 3–0 with Bobby Lennox among the scorers that night. So we were in the final and looking for our first win in the competition since 1954 when Jock Stein had been the Celtic captain!

In the four league matches before the final we inspired little confidence: we lost 6–2 to Falkirk at Brockville! And the Saturday before Hampden we lost 2–1 to Partick Thistle at Parkhead.

The best thing that happened to us in the build-up was being taken to a small hotel at Largs. Jimmy Steel – known as Steely – accompanied us in his role as masseur but even more importantly as court jester. Steely is a great guy to have with the squad – especially in a bad patch. He organizes all kinds of activities and that week he got together a putting competition which took on the significance of the Open Championship at St Andrews. He had the blackboard out on the lawns and began quoting odds. I think I was 12–1 against because I was up against Stevie Chalmers – a tremendous golfer. All the lads started backing me to put the wind up 'Steely' and incredibly I started hitting impossible putts right into the hole. I won the dinner set Steely had put up as the first prize and he had to pay out a fortune!

So the great day dawned at last and with morale high we set off for Hampden. I don't remember much about the hours leading up to the match or even arriving at the ground. But I do remember during the first half that my legs were like lead. Years later a doctor explained that it was sheer tension which drained my strength.

At half-time we were trailing 2–1 and it was the second time in the match that we had been a goal behind. Dunfermline had struck right on half-time so the dressing room was like a morgue. It was at that moment we saw Stein in action as the motivator. He coaxed us and encouraged us without a hint of recrimination towards any player, yet there would be times later that we'd go in at half-time 3–0 up and get a roasting.

Anyway my legs were lighter as we ran back onto the

pitch with the message ringing in our ears that it was 'just a matter of time'.

Well, we were young and determined and a matter of time it was! Bertie Auld had got our first half goal and he was also to get number two with some help from me. We played a couple of 1-2s and I cut the ball into his path from the left and it was 2–2. Then with minutes remaining I got the ball and started taking it wide. Jock had told me to do this and tire their defenders. I won a corner kick and from Charlie Gallagher's cross Billy McNeill headed a dramatic winner to end the years of famine.

Naturally the fans went mad. It was a dream come true and they lined the streets in their tens of thousands all the way from Hampden to the centre of Glasgow where we were holding the victory celebrations. At one stage Bertie Auld put his arm out of the window to shake hands and it took half a dozen of us to pull him back in. They stood outside the Central Hotel for hours and refused to go home until we held the Cup out of a window to tremendous cheers. It had been an unforgettable day.

Just four days later we were on our way to East End Park to face Dunfermline again – this time in a postponed league match. It was a game we could have done without, even had the opposition not been Dunfermline. They really had it in for us and cuffed us 5–1. It was a night where everything went wrong and we even missed a penalty when it was 0–0.

You should have heard Jock Stein at the end. You'd have thought we had lost the Cup. He began shouting and bawling but I thought I would be safe as he had given me a lot of praise for setting up two of the goals on the Saturday. But my turn came and I learned at that moment that the Cup final was very much in the past and he was talking about the present and the future. I just sat, head bowed, afraid to look up at the huge frame towering over me. When I thought he was finished I headed for the bath. But he wasn't! 'Where do you think you're going?' boomed the voice. 'Don't move till I've finished.' When he had said his piece none of us was in any doubt about the standards which would be demanded from that point on.

Following that experience the summer break was a very welcome one. There was no close-season tour although several matches were set up shortly after we resumed training in July 1965.

The previous month the ever-alert Stein had signed the Motherwell striker who had given us such a rough time in the Scottish Cup semifinals – Joe McBride. It was a tremendous signing for us because Joe was a great centre-forward and he joined us for the opening pre-season game against his old club on the Isle of Man. It was a match of no great distinction and we had to thank Stevie Chalmers for getting a goal near the end to give us a 1–1 draw. From there we went on to play Shamrock Rovers in Dublin and I scored twice in a 7–0 rout. But it was the following match which gave us the hint that we might be on the verge of great things. We travelled to Roker Park to play Sunderland who were parading their new signing, Jim Baxter from Rangers – a man who had enjoyed supremacy in the recent past when the Ibrox club dominated Celtic. Well, he was the one on the receiving end on his debut; we thrashed them 5–0. It was a real drubbing and I enjoyed my goal that afternoon. That set us up with a good start to the season – especially in the League Cup where we reached the semifinals in one of the most dramatic nights of my long career.

I suppose I scored a few vital goals in my time but on 4 October 1965 I hit a real lifesaver against Hibs at Ibrox. We were trailing 2–1 and well into injury time and I was beginning to think we'd had it. I remember the Hibs captain Pat Stanton – who was to join Celtic briefly more than a decade later – shouting to his men, 'We didn't come this far to throw it away.' Then big Tam Gemmell came galloping up the left in that famous style of his and we all knew it was the last chance. He cut along the by-line and I just hoped he would try and find me with the ball. But he had a shot which was blocked by the keeper. The ball broke to me but there was only the tiniest gap between him and the fullback. I lashed out and couldn't believe that I found that gap as the ball hit the net. We all went crazy because the whistle went immediately. Extra time was an anti-climax but we'd forced a replay. Hibs knew they had blown it and in the replay we had a convincing 4–0 win.

That goal was so important in many ways – and not just because I scored it. For years Celtic teams had floundered in the competition and for years had failed to qualify even for the quarterfinals. It meant the chance of continuity of success following the Scottish Cup win and I believe that had we lost to Hibs it could have badly dented our morale in the league championship which we were to go on and win that season.

So we found ourselves in the final against Rangers – a team which in those days had always had the beating of Celtic in cup finals. But this one was to be different in many ways.

For a start we got two penalty kicks awarded by referee Hugh Phillips and big John Hughes scored with both of them to give us a 2–0 lead at half-time. Big Yogi had a great game that day and fairly roasted Rangers' Danish right back Kai Johansen. John Greig got a consolation goal for Rangers near the end just to keep us on our toes till the final whistle but we were never in any real danger of losing.

Hugh Phillips pointed towards the South Stand and within months I had a League Cup winners' medal to add to the Scottish Cup medal. On the way to collect the cup I felt a little shiver go down my spine as I thought back to that injury time goal against Hibs!

We were very elated as we ran back onto the field to display the trophy but once again dreadful scenes were to mar a Hampden Cup final after a Celtic victory. Our intention was to take the Cup round the track at the Celtic end and then cut back along the half-way line to the dressing room. There was never any intention of taking it further. But before we reached the line it happened. I was sharing a laugh and a joke with another player when I heard, 'For God's sake, look.' A horde of blue-and-white clad fans were streaming towards us like a scene from *Zulu Dawn* and not for the first time in my life I was glad of my pace. I reached the safety of the tunnel first and as I looked round I saw Neilly Mochan and Tam Gemmell having to protect themselves with a few well-placed punches.

Obviously the scenes took away from the occasion but the important thing to us as players was that we had another trophy in the cupboard. The most disappointing aspect of the crowd misbehaviour was that laps of honour were banned for more than a decade depriving Celtic fans of seeing many trophies during the club's greatest era.

We went on to a celebration party that night although trophies were to become so commonplace that eventually it was a matter of 'just disperse from here, lads'. Personally I'm against the planned victory dinners because when it all goes wrong on the park there's nothing worse than a 'defeat dinner'. And we had a few of those as well. People would sit looking at their watches every few minutes and sighing just wishing it was time to go home.

With the League Cup on the sideboard we concentrated on the championship plus a good run in the European Cup Winners' Cup. We accounted for Go Ahead Deventer of Holland, Aarhus of Denmark and Kiev Dynamo of Russia to reach the semifinal of the tournament for the second time in two attempts. Suddenly we found ourselves billed in a Battle-of-Britain role against Liverpool with the first leg at Celtic Park. A huge crowd saw us pile on the pressure but at the end of ninety minutes we had only one goal – which I scored – to show for all our efforts and we realized it would be an uphill struggle at Anfield.

The second leg was played two weeks later – 19 April 1966 – and was to end in bitter disappointment and crowd trouble. We found ourselves down 2–0 although we hadn't been playing badly. The breaks had gone against us with John Clark diverting one of the goals past Ronnie Simpson when the ball came off his toe. We kept plugging away and near the end I scored the goal which should have kept us in the tournament, only for the referee to chalk it off. It was unbelievable. Joe McBride had set up the chance and I had carried the ball past the fullback Byrne before side-stepping the goalkeeper and placing it in the far corner. As the final whistle sounded a hail of cans and bottles landed on the park and, while you can never condone that sort of behaviour, the Celtic fans must have felt cheated.

The Liverpool players were overjoyed but even they admitted that we'd been robbed and one put an arm round my shoulder and said, 'Don't blame your fans. They paid a lot of money to come here and they've been robbed.' That's how obvious it was that the French referee had made a blunder. A couple of weeks later – back on the safety of his own soil – the referee had the nerve to admit in a magazine interview that he had made a mistake! There's no doubt in my mind that his decision that night cost Celtic more than £100,000 because the final was due to be played at Hampden Park where Liverpool eventually lost to West German opposition.

Some people have the theory that missing Hampden was a blessing in disguise; that, had we won the European Cup Winners' Cup, it could have gone to our heads and we might not have done so well in 1967 – the year we were to win the European Champions' Cup, championship, Scottish Cup, League Cup and Glasgow Cup. It's true that after we reached the pinnacle in Lisbon we crashed out of the European Cup in the very first round the following season. But I don't hold with the opinion that success in the Cup Winners' Cup would have dulled our ambitions. We were a young team which didn't know the meaning of the word pressure and it would have been tremendous to have won European tournaments two years running.

Another disappointment for me from the Liverpool experience came in the shape of an injury I'd picked up after a tackle by Ron Yeats, their Scottish centre-half. It kept me out of the Scottish Cup final against Rangers which ended 0–0 on Saturday. And there was further disappointment for me when just before the replay, Jock

Stein said he wouldn't gamble on my fitness and left me out. In the event it was a bad night for the club with Rangers winning 1–0 thanks to a goal from right-back Kai Johansen.

In the space of weeks we had taken a couple of hefty blows in two prestigious tournaments, but we had managed to keep our heads up in the championship race and at the end of the day that was the one we really wanted to win. It had been twelve long years since the championship trophy had been won by Celtic and the supporters were in party mood when we headed for Motherwell and the last game of the season. We needed only to avoid a 4–0 defeat to clinch the title and Rangers that morning had already sent a telegram of congratulations conceding the battle was over. I always wondered if that had been done to unnerve us? It certainly was a very nervy occasion and we had to wait till the very end before I scrambled the ball over the line to give us a 1–0 victory and an outright points win.

It was a scrappy goal in a scrappy game – the ball coming off my shin into the net – but it's one I'll always remember. Another memory from that day was travelling back in the team bus. We were all in deep conversation about the future when Billy McNeill said, 'Listen, lads, if we stick together we'll have the makings of a right good team that could really go places.'

And places we started going! We headed off for a holiday in Bermuda and played a couple of games against local opposition before heading for the States and Canada and real tests against class opposition. We went on to play eleven games undefeated with eight victories and three draws. And Bobby Lennox started to believe that he could be a goalscorer with nineteen strikes in those eleven matches. Bermuda was a dream and really gave us all a chance to mix and get to know each other. Morale was sky high and I'll give you an example of two of the laughs we shared as we formed into a real family team.

We were there only a couple of days when my buddy Jimmy Johnstone and I bought a couple of 'Texas-style' hats to make us look a couple of big shots! We had decided to mosey along to the room shared by Billy McNeill and John Clark to show off our purchases. Billy looked really impressed as he took the hat from my head then with a grin and a flick of the wrist sent it spinning across the room, over the balcony and down eight storeys! I remained calm and casually picked up a book by his bedside and inquired, 'Enjoying this Billy?' Before he could reply I had sent it spinning in the same direction as my hat. He froze in his tracks with a look of horror on his face and I remember thinking, 'It can't be that good a book'. John Clark flew past me onto the balcony and as I ran to look over it was raining five pound notes. Billy's entire holiday money had been hidden in the pages!

Billy and I took off downstairs like fiends while John kept a watchful eye on a little local lad who'd started gathering the cash thinking that Christmas had come early. Luckily for me we retrieved all of it and Billy lived up to his reputation for generosity by giving the little fellow half a crown!

Daft moments like that and the fun of adding yards to them at mealtimes brought about great friendships and things just got better and better. We found we were battling harder for each other on the field and getting closer to one another off it.

When we moved on to New York Big Jock warned us about the Big Apple at night and we had instructions to go out in groups of no less than four. I went out with Bobby Murdoch, wee Jimmy, Charlie Gallagher and Willie O'Neill. As we approached Times Square the hairs were standing on the back of my neck, then from a particularly dark doorway there was a scream and someone jumped out on top of me. My heart just about stopped until I realized it was Bertie Auld up to his tricks. He'd walked on and waited till I had strayed slightly from the main pack!

Bertie was great on the trip and it had been at that stage that Jock decided to convert him from a traditional winger to a midfield role along with Bobby Murdoch. It meant the likes of Stevie Chalmers and me having more freedom up front and the service from both of them was quite magnificent.

There was another drama at St Louis when a journalist appeared by the swimming pool. He saw the intent in our eyes but before he could escape we had him in the air and straight into the swimming pool. With that piece of work successfully carried out we all decided to go into the bar for a well-earned Coke only to see Sean Fallon rushing past and diving to the rescue. It hadn't occurred to us that the poor bloke couldn't swim!

When we got to San Francisco our chairman Bob Kelly was particularly pleased that we had beaten Tottenham Hotspur and we were all taken out for a slap-up meal. Mr Kelly asked us what we would like to eat and got the stock answer from footballers, 'Steak, steak and more steak.' When the meals were served up we were all astonished to see that among the thirty or so steaks was a plate of corned beef and cabbage. The chairman could see the looks on our faces but everyone was too afraid to say what they were thinking, 'Who ordered *that*?' He said simply, 'When people go to Scotland they sample haggis. San Francisco is famous for its corned beef and cabbage and that's what I'm having.' Bob Kelly was not someone you sniggered at. He was a tremendous man, if sometimes a bit distant. If he said good morning to you that was a sign of your having played well in the last game. He was a real Celt who thought only about the well-being and reputation of the club. If he had ordered thirty plates of corned beef and cabbage that night you can bet the mortgage we'd all have eaten it without a word.

It had been a fantastic tour for all of us and here are the statistics which prove that living, sleeping and eating football really does pay off:

| 12 May 1966: | Bermuda Select | 10–1 |
| 15 May | Young Men's Club, Bermuda | 7–0 |
| 18 May | New Jersey All Stars, Kearney, USA | 6–0 |

| 21 May | Tottenham Hotspur, University Stadium, Toronto | 1–0 |
| 25 May | Hamilton Primo, Hamilton, Canada | 11–0 |
| 27 May | Bologna (Italy) Roosevelt Stadium, Jersey City | 0–0 |
| 29 May | CYC All Stars, St Louis | 6–1 |
| 1 June | Tottenham Hotspur, Kezar Stadium, San Francisco | 2–1 |
| 5 June | Tottenham Hotspur, Vancouver | 1–1 |
| 9 June | Bayern Munich, Kezar Stadium, San Francisco | 2–2 |
| 12 June | Atlas (Mexico) Coliseum Stadium, Los Angeles | 1–0 |

Goals for, 47; goals against, 6

With that impressive record behind us we looked forward to 1966–7 with confidence yet not realizing that for all of us the greatest season of our lives was about to dawn. My nineteen goals on tour were to be a passport to full Scotland honours and the young, carefree boys who'd played games and pranks across a continent could all look forward to coming of age in spectacular style.

# 3

# 1967 and All That

The date was 6 June 1967 and we were sitting like raw youngsters in the majestic Bernabeu Stadium mesmerized by the skills of Gento and di Stefano. Phrases like 'that man's magic' and 'did you see that?' were buzzing about our group as we watched them with the ball at training.

Yet *we* were the champions of Europe, *we* had been invited to provide the opposition to the legendary Real Madrid, *we* had just won the grand slam and set some records Real must have envied.

But despite taking the crown which the Spaniards had held the previous season we were still in awe of names which had been making European history when some of us were just starting secondary school.

I tell this story to emphasize that having become the first British side to win the Champions' Cup just two weeks earlier, it had not and did not go to our heads. We had matured in a footballing sense in the long season which was just about to finish with the Alfredo di Stefano benefit match the following night – 7 June. But we were still the same happy-go-lucky boys who had set out for America a year earlier.

That tour, as I've often said, was the making of the team as we found out when we opened season 1966–7 against star-studded Manchester United on 6 August at Park-head. They were to win the European Cup after us in 1968 – but neither team knew of the glory ahead that afternoon. For us it was a splendid day with a convincing 4–1 win against Paddy Crerand, Nobby Stiles, Bobby Charlton,

Denis Law and George Best and I scored the opening goal of the season to give me a wonderful personal memory.

A couple of weeks later was another personal first for me when I hit a hat trick as we cuffed Rangers 4–0 at Ibrox in the opening round of the Glasgow Cup, making me the first Celtic player to score three goals there. A massive crowd of 75,000 saw Rangers miss a couple of early chances then we took over, and I remember hitting one of my best-ever goals. With Rangers captain John Greig snapping at my heels down the right, I wheeled and cracked the ball with my left foot high into the net.

John Greig was in opposition to me in countless Old Firm matches down through the years from the mid-sixties right through till he became manager of Rangers in 1978 and, despite his reputation, I enjoyed playing against him. He was a very fair player towards me and never really kicked me – although there was the odd foul! My ankle was broken in one match at Ibrox as he tackled me but I never blamed him for that and made it public in the newspapers. I always admired the way he did the best for his club in every game. He never really knew when he was beaten.

But he was to taste a few defeats at our hands in 1966–7 as we marched from trophy to trophy. On 17 September early goals by Bertie Auld and Bobby Murdoch gave us a 2–0 league win over Rangers at Parkhead and then we found ourselves going for a hat trick of wins in the League Cup final at Hampden on 29 October. We had shown spectacular form in the qualifying section, scoring 23 goals against Hearts, Clyde and St Mirren. We had beaten Dunfermline 9–4 on aggregate in the quarterfinals and beaten Airdrie 2–0 in the semis with Joe McBride showing his tremendous scoring power with fifteen goals.

The final itself wasn't a great game, we didn't play well despite being favourites. But it was a very special day for me because I scored the only goal of the game – my first-ever cup final goal. Bertie Auld found Joe McBride with a long, high pass and good old unselfish Joe who

41

might have had a go himself, nodded the ball into my path for a good clear shot at goal.

With so many good results by this stage in the season you might think that we fancied our chances for a clean sweep. But nothing was further from our minds. As players we never really sat and looked into the future. For a start, none of us knew if we'd be playing in the next game and we never really looked beyond the next game.

By early November we got the chance of trophy number two after beating Queen's Park 4–0 for the right to meet Partick Thistle in the Glasgow Cup final. And the night of 7 November brought it home to us that the paying customer is no mug when it comes to looking for value for money. We had beaten both Rangers and Queen's Park 4–0 and that was the scoreline at half-time against Thistle with me getting another hat trick. We left the field to thunderous ovation from the fans. But at full time it was still 4–0 and there was some booing and jeering as we went forward to get the Cup. Back in the dressing room Jock Stein said, 'What did you expect? You played in the first half but stopped in the second. Those people paid for ninety minutes of entertainment and didn't get it.' He was right of course but we didn't intentionally step off the gas. Being so far ahead we indulged in a lot of passing and a bit of the fancy stuff, but the biggest problem was that half-time had interrupted our flow. Quite often in games like that the interval was the worst thing that could happen. Yet had it been 0–0 at half-time we'd have been treated like heroes for a 4–0 win. It was a lesson, however, that the public call the tune – Cup win or no Cup win.

Everything, it seemed, was happening for me in these opening hectic months because November also saw me make my international debut. But more about that later.

By early December we had won ourselves a place in the quarterfinals of the European Champions' Cup at our very first attempt, having beaten Zurich 5–0 on aggregate with Tommy Gemmell scoring three and giving notice of the power he was to become on the European circuit. Nantes of France were next, we beat them on a 6–2 aggregate and I scored my first European Cup goals – one in each leg.

In the championship itself we were undefeated in all sixteen games and travelled to meet Dundee United at Tannadice on Hogmanay 1966 having gone a total of forty-eight games without defeat, and there's no doubt the strain of carrying that record about was beginning to tell. Everybody was out to stop our run and we had come from behind at places like Dunfermline to win 5–4 in the last minute with a penalty. Something had to give and it happened at Tannadice. They had a good side with seasoned professionals and beat us 3–2, although we almost got a point in a storming finish. I remember John Clark, known more for his fine defensive qualities, hit a tremendous shot just inches wide in the dying seconds just to prove that we didn't surrender anything lightly. But that defeat proved a blessing in disguise and we were to go right to the end of the league season suffering only one other defeat – again at the hands of United.

Fifteen games later they came to Parkhead on a sunny May evening and we had the chance to win the championship in front of our own crowd. Despite Celtic leading 2–1 they came back at us and won 3–2. They were the only Scottish side to beat us in fifty-three competitive games. They were simply a bogey team to us and the champagne had to stay on ice for another three days.

That defeat meant we could clinch the championship if we took a point against Rangers on the Saturday, and if we couldn't win it at Parkhead then Ibrox was certainly the next best place.

6 May 1967 saw rain pour from a leaden sky. Ibrox was bursting at the seams and the pitch was like porridge. But no matter how hard it came down it couldn't dampen the fire and fervour of our supporters who never even considered defeat. And neither did the Celtic players. There was no feeling of playing away from home and the pressures that could sometimes bring.

Helenio Herrera, the high priest of Italian catenaccio and coach to the great Inter Milan, sat unsmiling in the

stand watching us and weighing us up for our European
Cup final meeting which was then just nineteen days
away. He had already masterminded two European Cup
wins plus two victories in the World Club championship
for his ultra-defensive team. But what he saw that day,
before flying back to Italy in the club's private jet, must
have unnerved him. Both teams showed tremendous
stamina on the heavy pitch – not to mention a bundle of
skill and some fabulous goals. Sandy Jardine, just a
youngster playing one of his first games, gave Rangers the
lead with an out-of-this-world shot which found a tiny gap
and gave Ronnie Simpson not a chance. But as often
happens in Old Firm matches, there was an equalizer
within sixty seconds and I had a foot in it. There was a
scramble in the goalmouth and I got my toe to the ball
only for it to cannon off the post. But out of the corner of
my eye I saw Jimmy Johnstone dart in from the right to
score. At that moment I knew the title was ours and the
singing and dancing at the Celtic end at half-time seemed
to confirm that thought.

Fifteen minutes from the end we took the lead, yet it was
a goal I almost wished away. Thank God I didn't have the
power of mind over matter. Jimmy Johnstone had picked
the ball up some twenty-five yards out and started
running across the face of the penalty area with several
Rangers players moving in on him. I saw the Wee Man
was shaping up to have a crack but I couldn't believe he
would even contemplate one from that range in those
conditions as the mud tugged at his sparrowlike legs. I
was saying to myself, 'Don't hit it, don't hit it,' when he
unleashed a superlative shot which almost took the roof
out of the net. It was incredible.

Rangers would now have to score two to keep the
championship alive and for us it was just a matter of
playing it cool to the end. Rangers got one back through
Roger Hynd but there was never any panic in the ranks.
And in any case we had the cushion of a final league game
against Kilmarnock at Parkhead. The final whistle
sounded and it was a fabulous feeling. We had captured

the treble of championship, League Cup and Scottish Cup for the first time in the club's history. It was also the first time the league had been retained by Celtic since 1917.

As we walked from the field I shared a laugh and a joke with Willie Johnston which was captured in a newspaper photograph and surprised one or two people. This is as good a time as any to speak about the man who's made more headlines than most – many times for the wrong reasons. I always got on well with him on the field, I know over the years he's earned himself a reputation for upsetting the fans, but that's the sort of person he is. Players have a different relationship with each other than with fans and it's sometimes hard for the man on the terracing to appreciate this.

While never socializing with them, my relationships with Rangers players over the years have been good. Having played against them for the best part of twenty years gives me the right, I believe, to give a sound judgement on their players. It's a bit of a myth that they verbally abuse Celtic players about religion during games. In fact my experience was that players from some other clubs were, from time to time, really bitter against Celtic. I was called a Fenian so-and-so and that sort of thing but never once in my career was such a remark made to me by a Rangers player. Sure I fell out with a few of them during games and fairly heated words were exchanged, but never more than colourful language. I suppose I was luckier than most when it came to that type of abuse, or being kicked. I'd get tripped or have my jersey pulled but was never really subjected to the hard, dirty stuff that sometimes goes on. Maybe it's because I never got personally involved. To me getting on with the game was the only thing that mattered. Anyway the championship was won in some style with 58 points taken from a possible 68.

At the same time as we had been collecting those points we had been going strongly in the Scottish Cup and the European Cup. The Scottish Cup campaign had started on 28 January 1967 with a comfortable 4–0 home win over

45

Arbroath. But the memory of that day was not the result of any of the goals. Late in the second half we noticed the crowd stirring for no apparent reason. It began in the stand and spread like wildfire across both terraces before the roars collided in the middle of the Jungle with the impact of an atomic explosion. Bobby Murdoch turned to the Jungle crowd and got the message that Rangers had been sensationally beaten by Berwick Rangers at Shielfield Park, which will forever be known as the biggest shock in the history of the tournament. We went on to beat Elgin (7–0) with me getting a hat trick, Queen's Park (5–3) and we needed two games (0–0 and 2–0) against a stubborn Clyde side in the semis to reach Hampden once more and a meeting with Aberdeen.

We met the Dons on 29 April, just four days after reaching the European Cup final thanks to a draw against Dukla Prague. The fans gave us a tremendous reception and reaching Lisbon seemed to give our play a new maturity. Many of our supporters believe to this day that our performance against Aberdeen was one of the best ever. Our passing was tremendous and at one stage in the second half we unconsciously did a training routine where five or six of us indulged in knocking the ball forward and running to the back of the queue. As I said, it was completely unconscious and when we realized what we'd done there were a few contented smiles.

Willie Wallace, who had been signed just before Joe McBride dropped out through injury, scored both goals that day. The goals couldn't have been better timed with one just before half-time which I set up following a short corner from Bertie Auld and the other just after the interval which was made by Jimmy Johnstone. It certainly wasn't the hardest game of the season yet Aberdeen had provided us with stiff opposition in the league with drawn matches at Pittodrie and Parkhead. It was just that our teamwork that day made it impossible for them to compete. As I've said, that victory had come a mere four days after we had qualified for the European Cup final thanks to a nail-biting 0–0 draw against Dukla Prague in their Juliska Stadium. It was a performance which brought us a lot of criticism.

In the quarterfinals we had also been involved in a nail-biter against the strong Yugoslavs of Vojvodina Novi Sad. They had beaten us – our only defeat in the European campaign – by 1–0 on their own ground and held out well in the return at Parkhead in early March 1967. Their goalkeeper, Pantelic, looked set to break our hearts but, urged on by 75,000 fans, Steve Chalmers equalized the aggregate score after an hour. From then on in it was a siege and who will forget those final few seconds when Charlie Gallagher – in for Bertie Auld – struck the perfect corner kick onto the head of Billy McNeill for victory and surely one of Parkhead's greatest nights.

The first leg of the semifinals against Dukla saw Celtic take the field without me. A few days earlier at Seamill Jock Stein had driven up in his car and told me I had been chosen for Scotland to play against World Champions at Wembley. Then he promptly told me I was dropped from the Celtic team! His reasons were probably tactical and I was in no position to complain as the team won 3–1 at Parkhead with a goal from Jimmy Johnstone and two from Willie Wallace.

I duly played against England and scored in our 3–2 win to inflict their first defeat as World Champions and I was back in the Celtic side for the second leg in Czechoslovakia.

The real work had been done at home but the loss of the goal to a player called Strunc had us on edge. One goal from them in Prague and we knew that we could be in trouble.

I honestly can't remember Jock Stein instructing us to defend in depth. It was a case of us being pushed back as the game went on with the 36-year-old Josef Masopust pulling the strings. Wee Jimmy and I had been instructed to carry the ball wide and then deep into their territory and try to force throw-ins and corners, but I remember the way things turned out and that I was back alongside Tommy Gemmell for much of the game.

47

We had not made a bad start but obviously the nerves were getting to us because we knew we had come so close to making history, so close to being the first British team to reach the final. The atmosphere was a bit unreal as well.

I never really enjoyed playing in Eastern European stadia; the crowds reacted strangely to happenings on the field and there would be long periods of silence. I remember two real frights that afternoon. Just before the interval one of their players wheeled and hit a tremendously powerful shot. There were iron tubes running along the base of the nets and I heard the ball crash against metal giving off a real ping. I shouted, 'Oh no,' in the certainty that we'd lost a goal at a vital time. But as I opened my eyes again I saw the ball had hit the outside of the nets! Then Bobby Murdoch went down in a heap with one of their players in our penalty area, only for the referee to wave 'play-on'. At that moment I felt for the first time that we were safe.

We took a fair bit of stick from some sources over our performance but if ever there was a case for the ends justifying the means then this was it.

Everything was happening so quickly for me at that stage of the season that it was difficult to take it all in and realize what was being achieved. A Wembley appearance and victory against England, a league championship win – the first time the club had retained the title since 1917 – a Scottish Cup win to add to the earlier triumphs in the League Cup and Glasgow Cup ... and now a European Cup final appearance. Would this last victory come along and complete a most incredible fairy tale?

Seamill on the Ayrshire coast – our favourite retreat – was used for the preparations in the days before we flew out to Lisbon for the greatest memory of my football career. Perhaps the most relaxed man in the magnificent Palacio Hotel in Estoril was Jock Stein – certainly that's the impression he gave all of us. His planning had been meticulous and he fussed over us, making sure we stayed out of the sun. I remember for instance our reserve keeper John Fallon getting a bit of a telling off for letting

A training tussle with Jock Stein

Bertie Auld makes it 2-2 from my return pass in the 1965 Scottish Cup final against Dunfermline *(below)* and is congratulated by Steve Chalmers and myself

*Above* The Celtic squad pictured at a freezing Moscow airport during the trip to Russia to play Dynamo Kiev in the European Cup Winners' Cup, January 1966

*Opposite above* My first cup final goal and it's the winner in the 1-0 defeat of Rangers in the 1966-7 League Cup final which set us on the road to the grand slam

*Below* My first-ever goal against Rangers. It was the first of a hat trick as we beat them 4-0 in the 1966-7 Glasgow Cup at Ibrox

*Below* We beat Aberdeen 2-0 in the 1967 Scottish Cup final four days after playing in Prague to reach the European Cup final, and with the same team that was to play in Portugal the following month. *Left to right* Bob Rooney (physiotherapist), Willie Wallace (scorer of both goals), Jim Craig, Steve Chalmers, Bertie Auld, Jimmy Johnstone, Billy McNeill, Jimmy Steel (masseur), John Clark, Tommy Gemmell, Sean Fallon (assistant manager). *Front kneeling* Bobby Lennox, Bobby Murdoch, Neilly Mochan (trainer)

Celebrating at the Juliska Stadium after beating Dukla Prague 3-1 on aggregate to become the first British side to reach the European Cup final. *Left to right* Bobby Murdoch, Billy McNeill, Bertie Auld, Bobby Lennox, Steve Chalmers, Tommy Gemmell

Two of my great heroes. Denis Law *(left)* — his reflexes and courage were unmatched, his pace electrifying. Jimmy Greaves — a very special talent, the king of goal scorers.

the hot sun peep in through a gap in the curtains!

One of the things that helped us was that despite being fifteen miles from Lisbon there was a constant stream of fans looking for autographs and photographs. We really got the feeling of the importance of the occasion and the supporters were tremendous. They also appreciated the situation and didn't overdo things with their requests. On the afternoon of the game we were ordered to bed for a couple of hours. Jimmy Johnstone and I were sharing a room as usual and we were lying there chatting.

The Wee Man suddenly said, 'Inter Milan, what chance have *we* got?' It wasn't really said in a defeatist kind of way. What he meant was that they had twice won the European Cup and had also triumphed in the World Club championship and Jimmy was really looking for assurance.

I knew that Jock Stein felt we wouldn't have had much chance against the Italians over two legs and that prompted me to say to Jimmy, 'Look, it's eleven against eleven in one game and anything can happen.' And I added that Herrera would be worried about our pace and stamina after having seen us in the mud at Ibrox. Jimmy was a real worrier and I think it was good for him that we shared a room abroad because I could help relax him with a bit of patter.

The next thing we knew we were tucking into some steaks – which had been brought from Glasgow. Then we were on the bus for the stadium. The journey was to turn into a bit of a nightmare because of traffic jams and our driver taking a wrong turning which meant that we got to the Estadio Nacional just thirty-five minutes before kickoff time. In a way it turned out to be a bit of a blessing because we barely had time for a look at the pitch before getting stripped for the match. Some of the players took a cold shower because we were going out into eighty degrees of heat. What reassured us in those last few minutes when players get nervous was the fantastic support we had with us. When we had gone out to examine the pitch it had been like walking onto Parkhead!

Funny things race through your head before a match – especially an important match. I suppose I was reassuring myself as I looked back to the previous afternoon in the same Estadio Nacional. The Inter players had just finished training when we arrived, but these highly paid stars from a millionaire club waited behind to watch us go through our paces. That had been a compliment.

Yet Big Jock, master of psychology, had used the session to confuse them. I was put in a defensive role with John Clark the main striker! The Italians must havé been wondering what was so funny as we all had a good laugh. In many ways, our few days in Lisbon had brought back to us the memories of the American tour; no matter how important the match we were about to play, we had all decided to go out onto the pitch with two intentions – to enjoy ourselves and to do our best for Celtic and our magnificent supporters.

Jock too always thought of the fans, and among his last words to us before we left the dressing room were, 'How much do you think it cost those boys out there to get here today? You've got to get out there and do something for them. Some of them have probably worked a year's overtime to come here when they could just as easily have watched it on television.'

Jock knew how to get the adrenalin running all right!

As we left the dressing rooms we were met by Jock who told us he'd just been given the Inter team list – without the name of the great Luis Suarez. In the weeks leading up to the game Helenio Herrera had been involved in a war of nerves with Jock and their midfield genius had been written off by the Italian manager because of injury. But with the Italians you never knew what they were likely to spring. Jock was still wary and told us, 'Wait till we see them in the tunnel and then I'll believe it.'

At that point a light aircraft was circling over the stadium dropping advertisement leaflets and I think I was half expecting Suarez to parachute from it onto the centre-spot. But when we got to the tunnel he wasn't there and we took the opportunity to strike another psychological blow. Wee Jimmy and I started singing a few Beatles numbers and a lot of the lads – there were a few right good singers among the Lisbon Lions – joined in. Then as the West German referee Kurt Tschenscher led us from the semidarkness up a flight of stairs towards brilliant sunshine Bertie Auld started singing, 'Sure it's a grand old team' and you should have seen the looks on the faces of the Inter players. They thought we were madmen. But I felt ten feet tall.

Just seconds after the whistle which signalled the start of the twelfth European Cup final I experienced one of my strangest moments in football. Their player Bicicli – the replacement for Suarez – came running in my direction with the ball nowhere near us. He put his hands on my shoulders and then hugged me before sprinting away. It was nothing more than a friendly gesture – although puzzling that it should be done during the game! It certainly brought home to me that perhaps after all, these Inter supermen were human too despite their vast experience at this level of football.

It's history now that within eight minutes a penalty had been given against Jim Craig when the Inter player Renato Cappellini went down in the area. My reaction was sheer disbelief and I thought, 'Surely he can't give a penalty this early in a European Cup final.' But give it he did and Sandro Mazzola scored to give us a real uphill battle. With their reputation for defensive play the last thing we wanted to do was give them an early start. The referee's decisions that evening were strange to say the least. At one stage in the second half goalkeeper Sarti held Willie Wallace round both ankles in full view of the ref who proceeded to give a free kick yards away at a spot the ball hadn't been in.

Yet when big Tam Gemmell hit the equalizer from the edge of the box I was in an off-side position along with at least one other player. But it was such a magnificent shot there would have been a riot had he disallowed it. Certainly none of us were interfering with play and no goalkeeper – even the inspired Sarti – could have stopped the shot.

He continued to make breathtaking saves, including a spectacular one-handed effort from a Bobby Murdoch try, but the longer the game went on the more I believed we couldn't lose. The great defender Giacinto Facchetti began to sag after the equalizer and most of the Inter players seemed to lose their strength. I could sense they were tiring fast because I was going past them more easily, had there been extra time I'm sure we'd have got five or six goals.

It wasn't a final which will be remembered for the play of the front men but we had played a major role that day. Our instructions had been to go on strength-sapping runs and draw people out of position to create openings for the fullbacks Craig and Gemmell and our midfielders Bobby Murdoch and Bertie Auld. Murdoch and Auld began to get the better of Corso, Bedin and Bicicli with their sweeper Picchi overworked at the back. The important thing from our point of view was the team effort and in the early stages I like to think that Wee Jimmy and I frightened the wits out of them. I remember getting in a good cross from which Jimmy almost scored with a header and the minute that happened Burgnich, who had been detailed to mark me, signalled to Facchetti to take over. It was obvious that I was too pacey for him so he switched his attentions to the Wee Man. Italian defenders don't take long to get themselves sorted out!

Anyway we continued to make room for the men from the back and it was not surprising that the winner came from a Bobby Murdoch shot which was cleverly deflected into the net by Steve Chalmers.

Facchetti was quoted the following day as saying, 'Many times I tried to get forward in the match, but when I played the ball and ran I did not get it back. Really we were five men against eleven.'

At last the final whistle sounded and people were pouring onto the pitch from all directions. John Clark and I fell on top of each other and suddenly I panicked. 'My teeth,' I thought, 'I must get my teeth.' So confident had I been of victory that I had taken my false teeth out onto the park with me – something I had never done before. I had decided I wanted them for the presentation and lap of honour. I had wrapped them in Ronnie Simpson's cap and as I looked goalwards I saw a delirious Celtic fan trying to run off with it as a souvenir. I may have been running for ninety minutes in 80 degrees of heat but you should have seen the sprint as I took off to retrieve the situation! There's no doubt that was the big disappoint-ment of Lisbon from a player's point of view. At the time it didn't seem so bad, but in the days afterwards it hurt that there had been no lap of honour. We found ourselves under siege in the dressing room and somebody said, 'Where's the European Cup? Did we actually win it?' The dressing rooms were shabby – and crammed with people. The L-shaped design with the showers breaking it into two sections meant that we couldn't all get together for a real celebration. Billy McNeill had to struggle through the crowds to collect the cup, then return around the outside of the stadium in a police car.

I had dreamed of climbing the massive stairway of that magnificent marbled arena – a symbol of Portugal's Fascist past – but instead I was sitting on the team bus on the way to the UEFA banquet. Again the gloss was taken off the occasion when the Inter team kept us waiting for about an hour. Eventually they were forced to come along. At the end of the meal we had an impromptu medal ceremony. Someone had handed Billy McNeill a box containing the winners' medals and he handed them out.

The following day we arrived back in Scotland to amazing scenes. All the way in from the airport people were lining the route and flying flags and banners from windows. An estimated quarter of a million turned out to greet us. At Parkhead we lapped the track on a lorry and showed off the cup; the crowd would have kept us there till midnight if we'd let them. They refused to go home and eventually we had to sneak out of a back door to get home to our wives and families.

Our season still wasn't quite finished.

The day before the European Cup final the legendary Alfredo di Stefano had arrived at our hotel in Estoril and asked if we would provide the opposition for his testimonial match. While it had been a long, hard and unforgettable season and this would be our sixty-fifth match, the players were all for it.

I heard at the time the financial guarantee offered to us wasn't too great and while chairman Bobby Kelly looked on the invitation as an honour, Jock Stein pointed out that as potential champions of Europe we should demand the rate for the job. Certainly Real Madrid didn't play benefit matches for chickenfeed and Jock got his way.

It turned out to be a tremendous occasion and anything but a friendly. At one stage one of the fullbacks came up behind me and belted me on the back of the head. Then Bertie Auld and Amancio got their marching orders for fighting. It was a pity about the ordering off because there was a tremendous amount of good football played in front of more than 100,000 people. It was like playing a second European Cup final in the space of a couple of weeks. The Spanish press had really built it into a bit of a grudge occasion claiming that Real – winners the previous year – were the rightful champions of the continent and that we had merely borrowed the crown. I can tell you we were pretty determined to prove them wrong on their own patch, we let them get away with nothing.

Just before kick-off time they informed us that we had to wear blue pants! But there was no way Jock Stein would tolerate such sacrilege of our colours. Real had wanted to play in their famous all-white strip but were told in no uncertain terms by the boss that they change or there was no game. We stood by and watched as they went onto the pitch in all-white but after they had posed for the official photographs they returned to the dressing rooms and pulled on blue shorts.

We didn't win just that point either. After they had given us a bit of a chasing in the opening spell with di Stefano being outstanding we emphasized our champion status by winning the match 1–0 and I got the goal – one I'll never forget. Jimmy Johnstone beat three or four men and gave me the pass as I came in from the right. It was a special feeling even though it was greeted with absolute silence. The stadium was so quiet that all I could hear were the voices of team-mates shouting, 'goal, brilliant, magic.' It was the final seal on a magnificent season and a result which could only enhance our reputation world-wide. To beat Real, the European Champions of 1966, on their own ground was no mean feat.

The result also meant that in sixty-five games we had suffered only four defeats – twice at the hands of Dundee United in the championship, once to the Yugoslav side Dynamo Zagreb in a friendly and once to their country-men Vojvodina in the European Cup.

It had been the season to end them all and we knew that things could only get harder for us because there was no way to follow an act like that. Five trophies … five victories. It had started way back on 6 August 1966 against Manchester United at Parkhead – themselves a team about to experience European Cup glory. I had scored the very first goal of the season in that match and as it turned out scored the very last against Real Madrid.

My total for the season comprised thirty-two competitive goals – thirteen in the league, seven in the Glasgow Cup, five in the Scottish Cup and another five in the League Cup plus two in the European Cup with the scores against United and Real bringing me a grand total and personal best to that date of thirty-four.

Jock Stein was quoted at the time as saying that the only thing Celtic hadn't won that year was the Derby and Bobby Lennox would have sped home in that had he been eligible!

As I said, the Real Madrid match was and always will be a special memory. After fifteen minutes di Stefano gave a pre-arranged signal to the referee and the match was stopped. A single spotlight picked him out as he ran up the stairway to embrace and be embraced by club president Santiago Bernabeu. Still under the piercing light he returned to the pitch to thank the players and I got his final handshake before he disappeared into the darkness and the referee restarted the game. One of the world's greatest players had departed and the stage was suddenly left to us. Somehow that seemed to sum up what we had achieved.

# 4

# Set to Quit Celtic

Only once in the thirteen years he was my manager did I see Jock Stein blush, and it happened many thousands of miles from home. We had just started our Far East tour of 1977 and for me it was a vital time in my career. Two nights earlier I had played my first full match since breaking my ankle against Rangers and had given the Singapore XI a bit of a roasting. This particular evening we were attending a big function when Jock informed us our match was about to be shown on TV in an adjoining room, so the players went through to watch.

The Big Man sat down beside me on a two-seater settee and we all settled down to admire ourselves. Bertie Mee, the former Arsenal manager, was also on tour in the area with the Highbury club and sitting alongside the commentator giving his opinions. At one stage I had burst past two defenders to create a chance and he commented, 'Yes, Bobby Lennox is still a valuable member of the Celtic pool.' And his next sentence devastated me! 'I once offered a British record fee for him.' I was blushing and too afraid to look at the Big Man but when I did he was blushing too and the players were nudging each other and tittering away in the background.

Jock had never cracked a light about it in the past but what he didn't know was that not only Arsenal had been showing interest in me in the late sixties. Everton and Tottenham Hotspur also put out feelers in my direction. Bertie Mee could have been talking through a hole in his hat that evening but Jock didn't deny it and he was the type of man to say something like, 'Don't believe a word of that,' if it wasn't true. Was I angry that I hadn't been consulted about what would have been a massive transfer fee? Not a bit. In fact I was flattered that Celtic and Big Jock obviously thought so highly of me that they turned it down. To be honest no other club ever interested me. But there was one occasion when I decided to quit Celtic – less than nine months after we had won the European Cup.

Just weeks after our Lisbon glory and the di Stefano benefit match in Madrid I got married to a local Saltcoats lassie called Kathryn Murray.

We left on honeymoon for Ibiza where, believe it or not, the weather was chilly. I discovered that we could move to another hotel in Palma without losing our money, although we had to wait till we got back home for our refund. But who was it who said footballers aren't shrewd? The great di Stefano had given the players a cash gift plus a watch after his match and of course that meant there were a few pesetas floating around. I had paid some of the lads sterling, got a few bob together and paid it into a Spanish bank. So we still had funds and set off on the short flight to Palma. I made the mistake of going into the hotel on my own, leaving Kathryn in the car with our luggage. The senor at reception didn't want to know me when I asked for a double room. But once I produced wife and baggage he was quite happy. When we got settled in we decided to go for a walk and popped into a hotel for a drink only to meet Joe McBride, Bertie Auld, Billy McNeill all with their families and friends. What a honeymoon we had!

But like all honeymoons it had to end, and it seemed no time till we were back at Parkhead for pre-season training and preparations for the defence of five trophies.

We took only three points from our first three championship matches, losing the second to Rangers 1–0 at Ibrox. But amazingly that was to be our last defeat in the league for the rest of the season!

In the League Cup we went well too, accounting for a

tough section of Aberdeen, Dundee United and Rangers. We beat Ayr United 8–2 on aggregate in the quarterfinals and walloped Morton 7–1 in the semis. In the final against Dundee at Hampden I got my seventh League Cup goal of that season in our 5–3 win, the second year running I had scored in the final.

Indications were that another magnificent season lay ahead of us despite our shock first round exit from the European Cup earlier in that month of October. We had been caught cold by Russian champions Dynamo Kiev at Parkhead when they beat us 2–1 on a night where they broke away twice. I pulled a goal back to give us some hope in the return leg two weeks later. We were still proud champions of the Continent and not ready to relinquish our crown without a fight.

Yet although we put up a fine performance we were victims of a dreadful Italian referee who gave us nothing. Russia turned out to be an unreal experience in many ways. For instance, about 10,000 people would turn up to watch us train, and in the streets people would hassle you all the time wanting to buy your shirt or jeans or anything you happened to be wearing.

I remember in the first half of the match we were very composed and confident and had the Russians on the run. A ball came over from the left which Willie Wallace just missed but which Billy McNeill, coming in at the far post, knocked into the net only for the referee to disallow it. Why, I'll never know. Even at half-time and still trailing 2–1 on aggregate, we were confident. We knew we were the better side. Big Jock was happy with our play and told us to carry on in the same manner. 'Just two goals, lads, that's all we need,' he shouted as we ran back onto the park.

but then came another blow. Bobby Murdoch, who had been booked for a trivial offence in the first half, was sent off for throwing the ball away. I know all of this sounds like sour grapes, but believe me, we got a raw deal. At last it seemed the breaks were coming our way when I got the aggregate equalizer to put us 1–0 ahead on the night. Bertie Auld provided the cross and everyone ran to mark Billy McNeill leaving me the chance. Still we pushed on and I broke clear with John Hughes with both of us on-side. I thought that Yogi would need help but he carried on, rounded the keeper and rolled the ball into the net. We were ecstatic until we saw the referee pointing to the ground and awarding a free kick to Kiev. It was unbelievable. And just to rub salt in the wound they broke away in the dying seconds to score and put us out on a 3–2 aggregate.

It was a crushing disappointment but nothing compared to what was about to happen next to Celtic Football Club – one of its blackest hours.

On 18 October – exactly two weeks after Kiev – we played the Racing Club of Buenos Aires for the World Club championship. The first leg was at Hampden and we had been told the South American champions were a pretty rugged lot. They kicked us, spat upon us, pulled our jerseys but didn't beat us. Billy McNeill headed the only goal of the match and we weren't at all impressed by them. As with Kiev, we knew we were a better side and I was confident of beating them in Buenos Aires.

That first leg cost me a Scottish cap against Ireland because one of their defenders had clobbered me on the ear and the club doctor ruled me out immediately after the match.

However that disappointment was behind me when we set out for the other side of the equator just hours after retaining the League Cup against Dundee. The party was in tremendous spirits as we set out on a tiring twenty-four-hour journey.

Big Jock was telling us on the way in from the airport that our accommodation was at a millionaires' country club and that we'd have everything we needed to get over the journey.

But when we arrived the Big Man hit the roof. It looked nice enough from the outside but inside it was incredible. Small rooms with peeling wallpaper, camp beds and small cookers. Jock sorted things out quickly and we were moved to premises in keeping with our status!

One rather unnerving aspect of the situation was the heavy guard around the hotel. They followed us everywhere in their spiked helmets. It was quite comical one morning when we went to Mass. They walked alongside us hitting anyone who pestered us with their batons and whips. Next thing they were kneeling all around us in the chapel!

It was the same when we left for the stadium later that day – 1 November 1967. The bus driver knew what he was doing when after several attempts he got the coach exit flush against the main doors of the stadium. There were thousands of Racing fans awaiting our arrival. They were spitting and jeering and being held back by a huge police presence. Mounted police belted them with whips while the ground force had Alsatians the size of horses on the end of long chains.

When we went out onto the pitch to have a look around the din was unbelievable. Thankfully there was a wide moat full of green slimy water – it wouldn't have surprised me if it had been filled with alligators! A policeman warned us to stay away from it because the fans could throw things at us at that range. Some of them were wearing only loin cloths as they raced up the high wire fences in menacing mood. It was comforting to know so many police were stationed about the place but unfortunately they didn't manage to give us total protection.

Just seconds before we kicked off, our goalkeeper Ronnie Simpson suddenly keeled over after being struck on the back of the head by a piece of metal which must have been catapulted from one of the fences.

We were stunned. Surely the tie would be awarded to us, not a chance! There was no way the referee would cancel the match in front of a crowd like that so Ronnie was carried off and John Fallon helped out of his tracksuit. One minute John had been sitting on the bench and then seconds later he was playing in the World Club championship. What was going through his mind is nobody's business but he was a brave man.

John Fallon was maligned by some people because of

one bad game against Rangers. In my opinion he was an excellent keeper. I thought Ronnie Simpson was the greatest but I had no fears about John taking over that day. Remember he had come into the team for the di Stefano match and played a blinder. He was a great reflex man. If John was in my goal then I was happy.

The early stages of the match saw us dominate but within seconds Wee Jimmy was knocked to the ground and I saw another player being kicked from behind and knew that it would be no picnic. Jimmy showed a lot of courage and scored a great goal after beating two men and the goalkeeper, only for it to be disallowed. But the Wee Man was in determined mood and again he got right through only to be pulled to the ground by the goalkeeper. It was such a stone-wall penalty that even this referee had to give it. I remember Tommy Gemmell running forward to take it in his own unmistakable style. But as he began his run so did the keeper and he must have met the ball about five yards from goal. But the power of Tam's shot was so great that the ball spun off his hands into the corner of the net and we were 2–0 ahead on aggregate and playing confidently.

Racing got one back before half-time. It was enough to make you weep, their player was a mile offside yet the score stood. Everyone had stopped except the referee and the Racing player.

Then during the interval we found ourselves the victims of further despicable tricks by the Argentinians. Jock was talking to us and quite happy with our play when he asked about oranges or juice for the players. There was nothing available and it was at this point that we discovered the water had been turned off in the showers. There can be no doubt it was a deliberate attempt to stop us freshening up for the second half, which was to be played in some considerable heat.

We sat and waited for the referee to knock on the door ... ten minutes ... fifteen minutes and then we were informed Racing were out on the pitch. In fact our break had been eighteen minutes and they had been back out on the field for about seven minutes with the crowd seething at our later arrival.

They equalized the tie in the second half and after that, it seemed, no one would win the game. They seemed happy to hold on and we just couldn't raise our game.

After the final whistle our chairman Bob Kelly came to the dressing room and he told Jock Stein, 'That's it, we fly home tomorrow.' But Jock knew the mood of the players. Despite being kicked by them for two matches we still felt we could win the tie and eventually we got our way.

We crossed the River Plate to neutral Montevideo in Uruguay for the play off on 4 November and Racing had a large support with them. But at least we had a chance of winning over the Uruguayans, although our pre-match attempt didn't quite work out. Just before kick-off time we set off down the tunnel carrying a Uruguayan flag and ran round the pitch to great cheers. But seconds later Racing appeared with a flag four times the size of ours! Again Ronnie Simpson was out – still not fully recovered from the trauma of Buenos Aires – as we lined up for what was to be a brutal encounter for the third time. Right from the start they began hacking and kicking and the safest place to be was on the ball!

The pitch was practically all baked mud with cracks throughout and the ball difficult to control. But I remember early on I got a break when the ball bounced for me and I reacted quickly with a Racing player moving in. But my shot was just inches over the bar and I often thought afterwards what might have been had that shot gone in. It would have sickened them. I don't blame myself because it was only a half chance, but if only . . .

Still early in the game there was a dust-up involving several players and the referee called the two captains together for a warning. Next thing I knew Billy McNeill was shouting to me, 'Watch it Bobby, he says the next incident and you're off the park. Watch yourself.' It was incredible. I hadn't been anywhere near the incident. A short time later Wee Jimmy went down after a horrendous waist-high tackle and all hell broke loose. The Racing keeper ran up the park, lifted the Wee Man and then belted him on the top of the head. A policeman came running on and clubbed the keeper with his baton and the Argentinian custodian ran off back between his posts.

I was on the fringe of this mayhem merely watching when the referee raised eight fingers, pointed at my number and sent me off. I was bemused and shattered as I walked off only to snap out of it at the sight of a towering inferno called Jock Stein. 'Where are you going?' he roared.

'I've been ordered off,' I replied.

'Get back on that field,' he barked in that gruff voice of his. So on I went again. The referee spotted me and again gave me my marching orders. Jock then threatened to boot my — for me and ordered me back on.

Meanwhile Racing were trying to do a deal with the referee, offering their number eleven who was injured and trying to hold onto their number six who had also been ordered off! When that was cleared up the referee spotted me lurking again and he called for a policeman who began drawing a sword. That was it! Jock Stein's boot or not I wasn't going to end up on the end of cold steel and I vanished up the tunnel.

I was still in the shower when the players came in at half-time. I just couldn't move and stood there weeping. Eventually I got dressed and headed down the large, wide tunnel and as I approached two huge, green swing doors I almost had a heart-attack. They burst open, almost coming off the hinges, and the man who came hurtling through was Jimmy Johnstone – also almost in tears.

'The — sent me off,' he yelled. 'One of their players grabbed my shirt and I threw up my arm to help get me clear and I was off,' said the Wee Man. He went on to tell me that the man who had tackled him went down as if poleaxed then got back to his feet wearing a bandage round his forehead. Those guys from the Racing dugout could have performed open-heart surgery on the centre-spot they carried so much gear about with them! And made the most of it.

As we consoled each other in the dressing room a Uruguayan official popped his head round the door to tell us Racing had scored. The afternoon was getting more disastrous by the second.

We went back down the tunnel to watch the remainder of the match just in time to see John Hughes get his marching orders after a clash with the goalkeeper and Bertie Auld too was sent off but somehow managed to stay on the park till the end.

We were all so despondent at full-time and I was wallowing in self-pity because of my ordering off. Defeat was bad enough but the manner in which we had lost was hard to accept. We knew word would be reaching home that players had been ordered off and that some people would think the worst of our behaviour.

The return journey was a nightmare. We were told we had to go back to Argentina and fly home from there. We were fogbound at Montevideo Airport and when we eventually got to Buenos Aires our crew had used up their hours and needed more sleep before going back on duty. While stranded at both airports for hours on end we had neither food nor drink. You can imagine the roar that went up when our plane touched down at Rome on the way home. We still had to fly to London and then Glasgow, but at least we were back on the continent where we were still reigning champions.

We heard afterwards from contacts of the club that I had been earmarked for an early bath because it was reckoned I was a big danger around goal. We also heard that the ballot for the choice of referee had been rigged. And in his autobiography my old mate Pat Crerand revealed that our referee from Buenos Aires was a linesman the following year when Manchester United were booted out of the same tournament by another Argentinian side, Estudiantes de la Plata, and Paddy commented in his book, 'If that bloke had the whistle that's why my old chums from Parkhead never had a chance.'

\*       \*       \*

I missed 5 games because of flu when we arrived home and fullback Jim Craig missed a few but thankfully we managed to keep going in the championship race going through November without losing a goal.

I got a couple of goals in an unbeaten December and scored in our 2–0 win over Hibs at Easter Road on 20 January 1968. It was seven days later that for the first time in my career I wanted to get away from Celtic. We were playing Dunfermline in the first round of the Scottish Cup at Parkhead and I turned up at the ground looking forward to the tournament and especially to the thought of retaining the Cup.

But in the dressing room I was shattered when Jock Stein came in and read out the team. I wasn't chosen. I didn't suffer from the superstar complex but I was genuinely upset at being dropped. Everyone in the team seemed surprised too, but the Big Man's word was law and he didn't have to give reasons. I went up into the stand, and to make matters worse we lost 2–0 in a bad match.

I drove home in a daze, but in my mind I kept saying it was time to leave Celtic, time to move on. I told my wife, my brothers and my father. None of them seemed to think it a good idea but the final decision had to be mine. Twelve months earlier I had been the happiest bloke in the world as we swept all before us. Now, it seemed, everything was going wrong . . . defeat in Europe, defeat in South America and out of the Scottish Cup.

On the Monday I drove back to Parkhead determined to go straight into Jock's office and give him the news. But as I walked towards the door my heart got smaller and smaller and I walked on into the dressing room. Tuesday was the same. By Wednesday I had convinced myself that I should leave it another few days and let Jock get over the disappointment of the previous Saturday. On Friday I again walked past his door on the way out and suddenly his head appeared. 'Come in Bobby, I want a word with you in the office,' he said. Before I could say anything he went on, 'Do you know why you didn't play last week?' I shook my head. 'Well,' he said, 'I thought the crowd atmosphere and the jerseys would have beaten them and I decided to play Joe [McBride] and Stevie [Chalmers] up front to give you a rest.' He added that he had felt I wasn't fit.

I had been getting some treatment for a foot injury earlier the previous week but had trained on the Thursday and Friday; I knew I was fit and told him so. It was at that moment that he broke with the habits of a lifetime and told me I was playing the following day. 'Now away home and get a good night's sleep,' he added. Whether he wanted me to have a rest or not I'll never know. But the thought that I was back in the team ended my brief spell of wanting to get away from Celtic.

To be honest, if Jock Stein had ever said I could leave I'd have burst out crying in his office. Celtic were always the only team for me.

From that day on everything, as they say, came up roses. The day after our talk I scored two goals against Partick Thistle at Parkhead in a 4–1 victory and I was to score a total of twenty league goals in the last twelve matches of the run-in – hitting the back of the net in each game. I got three against Aberdeen and four against St Johnstone as we demolished team after team.

Yet despite having lost only one game Rangers were still two points ahead of us and they were unbeaten. It was a tremendous race and something had to give – it did. They dropped a point to Dundee United and the break-through came for us on the night of 17 April 1968. We were playing Clyde in the Glasgow Cup final at Hampden while Rangers were playing a league match against Morton at Cappielow. At half-time we were 7–0 ahead and Big Jock followed us into the dressing room to tell us Morton were leading 2–0. We couldn't believe it. Some-times he would give us another team's score but he'd maybe switch it round to give us a fright and gee us up. But there was no jesting that night. During the second half we were more interested in looking towards our dugout than looking for more goals, and when Bobby Murdoch scored a spectacular eighth no one went particularly wild. As we went down the tunnel at the end with the Cup we heard it was 3–2 but not a final score. Then it was 3–3 and all over. Not only had we taken the Glasgow Cup that night, but taken over the league leadership on goal average.

Three days later at Parkhead we faced the same Morton and were soon to find out that their result against Rangers was no fluke. Although we took the lead early on through Willie Wallace they equalized through Joe Mason before the interval.

That early goal was probably the worst thing that could have happened to us and it took us a long time to get into top gear. The minutes ticked away in the second half as we mounted furious attacks and gave our supporters heart conditions. Into injury time and still the game was at 1–1. I ran over towards the Jungle at the Celtic end to take a throw-in and a fan shouted, 'Bobby, Rangers are winning 2–1 at Kilmarnock. They're going to win the league.' Suddenly I left the ball to someone else and sprinted into the middle. Over it came and Willie Wallace took a swipe and missed but I got a toe to it and poked it towards goal. Everything seemed to happen in slow motion because the keeper had seen the danger and hurled himself at me, but the ball just got under him and rolled into the net. We went crazy – but not until after I had raced back to the centre-spot to get away from any linesman that might have been tempted to raise a flag! We were still ahead on goal average and both Rangers and ourselves had just one game left. They had Aberdeen at Ibrox and we had to travel to Dunfermline needing both points to make sure.

As luck would have it, the Fife club had reached the Scottish Cup final after giving us the first round KO and that meant that we had a blank day on Saturday, 27 April – the last official day of the season. Jock took us to Seamill to prepare for the Dunfermline match, which was to be played the following midweek, and we travelled up in cars to watch the Cup final at Hampden.

Over at Ibrox, Rangers had the chance to turn the screw again by beating Aberdeen and leaving us with it all to do at East End Park. I left Hampden early – along with Jimmy Johnstone, Willie O'Neill, Charlie Gallagher and Bobby Murdoch – to head back for Seamill. Just a couple of miles past Lugton a radio announcer said, 'And the news from Scotland is that Dunfermline have won the Scottish Cup and Rangers have suffered their first league defeat of the season.' Wee Jimmy, who was driving, hit the brakes and the car almost landed in a ditch. We all leapt out dancing about, hugging each other and screaming like lunatics. Thankfully no one else was passing at the time. That's the road I take to and from Parkhead every day, and I never pass that spot without thinking about the championship and our unusual celebrations.

So it was on down the road to Seamill where we all met up for an unforgettable night. Although we still had to go to Dunfermline we'd have to have lost about 15–0, and that wasn't likely. But there was pride at stake as champions against Cup winners and we owed Dunfermline a beating after our first round defeat.

As it turned out, half of Glasgow travelled through to East End Park that night and it was pandemonium trying to get our bus up to the stadium. The size of the crowd was an all-time record for the ground and fans were everywhere – on floodlight pylons, stand and enclosure roofs and around the trackside. The atmosphere was as electric as anything I've ever experienced. Dunfermline scored first but we had a good spell of pressure. I remember one of our shots flying just wide and the sway amongst the crowd was so great that they came spilling onto the park. The next thing I knew a wee lad from New Stevenson was standing talking to me asking how I thought the game would go! It was that kind of night. I got one back and scored the winner near the end, and I felt a great satisfaction as I belted the ball into the roof of the net.

That one magic moment wiped out the memory of defeat in Europe, South America and the Scottish Cup. It also wiped out the memory of ever wanting to leave

Parkhead. It also happened to be my forty-fourth goal of the season and my thirty-second in the championship. It won me the European Bronze Boot from a French magazine in a competition based on league goalscoring. It seemed to be a high-scoring year in Europe because the great Eusebio of Benfica (43) and Antal Dunai of Ujpest Dozsa (36) took gold and silver.

Another season was over and, despite so many setbacks for the club, it had from a personal point of view, been my best season because of those goals. We had known twelve months earlier after our grand slam that things could only get harder for us. We had taken the League Cup and the championship and had gained a lot of new experience for the twelve months ahead.

# 5

# The International Scene

The 'Tartan Army' – Scotland's legions of fans – are a strange breed to say the least. Over the years, some have brought shame to the country, while others have enhanced the folklore and humour which surround some of the most colourful characters in world football.

My favourite moment – untold until now – came just minutes after my greatest international experience. We had beaten World Champions England at their own Wembley Stadium against all the odds and were lining up for the national anthem before heading off to the dressing rooms and our celebrations.

I was standing beside Denis Law as the band played 'God Save the Queen' and within seconds the place was teaming with our tartan-clad fans. One real rough-looking punter came up to Denis and forced a fiver into his hand shouting, 'Great, just great. Get the boys a drink, buy those boys a drink on me.' Denis tried to give it back but to no avail.

It's a tragedy that we have attracted so many of the wrong type of headlines over the Wembley fixture in the past decade because there's no doubt there are some great fans who just want to enjoy themselves – and as in the case of our benevolent friend – to share that enjoyment. My international career was short compared to many of today's players. I received ten full caps, including two appearances as substitute, and I enjoyed every minute of the experience between November 1966 and April 1970.

It was important to me to play for my country and, like

every player, the first cap was the one I really treasured. It meant that I could tell my children their daddy had been an internationalist and had played at the highest level.

It has been suggested several times through the years that Celtic players suffered when it came to handing out Scottish caps. The most recent rumblings came in the seventies when David Hay was dropped after winning a string of caps. Rangers captain John Greig was given a place in the team for the 1971 Wembley fixture – the only Ibrox player in the side – and the official reason for him replacing Davie was that he had more experience. Yet the previous season Davie had played in all three Home International matches and had also taken part in a European Champions' Cup final. A little later Kenny Dalglish found himself dropped on the eve of equalling the record number of consecutive caps by George Young of Rangers. Certainly these were two instances where questions could be asked. But for my own part I had no complaints. If I was chosen I played gladly. If I was left out it didn't upset me.

My debut came on 16 November 1966 in the Home Internationals against Northern Ireland at Hampden, and I couldn't have had a better start. There were six Celtic players in the side to help boost my confidence and it seemed to work. I cut back the ball to give Bobby Murdoch his goal and then I got the winner in our 2–1 victory.

If truth be told, I never saw the goal. I was facing the wrong way as Joe McBride headed down a cross from Willie Henderson of Rangers and I hooked the ball over my shoulder. The first I knew I had scored was when Billy Bremner grabbed a hold of me and the Hampden roar split the air. It was some feeling.

But it was nothing to what I felt when I won my second cap. As I said earlier, the first was the one to treasure but my selection against England at Wembley was to be the cap I'll never forget. They were Champions of the World and the previous summer had shown they were practically invincible on their own ground. We Scots didn't like the idea and set off south to end their unbeaten run.

I have a few memories in the hours leading up to kickoff that day. For instance I phoned Kathryn – still my fiancée at that time – and she told me she and her mum had both put a pound on Scotland. And it shook me when she said a lot of people had been putting money on me back in Saltcoats where the bookies were offering something like 8–1 against me scoring a goal. Thankfully I didn't have too much time to worry about that before we went off to the stadium. It was hard to believe, but the first person I saw as the team bus reached the top of Wembley Way was my dad. There he was sitting on the steps. My dad was the greatest – a quiet, modest man. He'd probably asked my uncle to collect the tickets I had arranged for him. He wouldn't go up to a door and ask. He spotted me and waved back. It made my day, not just knowing my dad was there at the match but that we'd seen each other.

Walking up the slight incline of the Wembley tunnel was one of the greatest moments I had in football. When I saw the masses of yellow flags and the Lion Rampant there was a lump in my throat.

The match itself was a great one for us, despite the fact that we were underdogs. When we had gone to look at the pitch the previous day the Chelsea fullback Eddie McCreadie had looked up at the giant scoreboard which read, 'England 0, Scotland 0' and he had turned to me and said, 'If it's still like that at twenty-to-five tomorrow I'll be wearing my Scotland jersey to Stamford Bridge on Monday morning.' No one really gave us a chance, yet when you look through the side we had players capable of anything. For a start there were my three Celtic team-mates – Ronnie Simpson making his international debut at the incredible age of thirty-six, big Tommy Gemmell and Willie Wallace – all just a month short of playing in a European Cup final. And we had the incomparable duo of Jim Baxter and Denis Law.

Jim Baxter was something special. I played on the same side as him three times for Scotland and loved every moment. The man's arrogance rubbed off on you immediately. He'd tell you the opposition were rubbish and you'd win. It was the same that day at Wembley. We won 3–2 and I scored the second goal after Denis Law had given us the lead. A free kick was cleared but hit back into the English area by Tam Gemmell and I hit the ball first time into the net. As I ran upfield I had two thoughts in my mind.

I kept thinking, 'My dad's seen me score a goal at Wembley,' and I was also over the moon for all the people in Saltcoats who were about to collect 8–1 from the bookies!

We should have made the scoreline greater that afternoon but even though England pulled back to 3–2 I could never see us losing. I had the feeling that if they scored again we'd go upfield and regain the lead. That's the sort of match it was for us.

The English centre-half, Jack Charlton, had got that second goal after limping to centre-forward after a clash with yours truly. He got the hero's treatment from the press the following day but they didn't know that I had taken the brunt of the tackle. He had a defective stud in his boot and when he had tackled me it caught my knee. It left me with a gaping wound and at the same time the impact had forced the stud through his boot and broken his toe! I managed to finish the match but carried the scar of that tackle for many a day.

Later that night the blood was still seeping from the wound through a thick bandage and all over my new grey suit trousers!

Before leaving the actual Wembley match I must tell you another few interesting stories. Did you know for instance that a good number of the Scotland players enjoyed a wee hauf before going onto the field? Bet you didn't! It all stemmed from a tradition at Celtic Park which eventually stopped early in the Stein era. There was always a cup full of whisky left in the dressing room before the match and players would take a sip just before going onto the field. The tradition wasn't part of the Scotland set-up but a player who shall remain nameless took a half-bottle into the Wembley dressing room. Tots were handed out on the quiet and players from other clubs joined in. It wasn't usually a thing I indulged in but there was one occasion when I realized the possible merits of a sip of the cratur before a match. We played Hearts in the Scottish Cup at Parkhead and just before half-time I had taken a real whack in the stomach. In the dressing room I thought I was going to vomit but Doc Fitzsimmons saved the day.

He handed me a cup and told me to drink it quickly. I thought it was some sort of medication but it turned out to be what I can only describe as a real belter! For the opening half-hour of the second half the effects were electrifying. I was everywhere and feeling great. But in the final fifteen minutes my legs turned to lead. I'm not advocating players should take up drink before a match, but there could be something in having just a wee sip!

That particular memory had come from just before the game. The next one came at the end. Jimmy Greaves was one of my great heroes and it had been a great thrill to play against him that day. I had met him when I had gone to Chelsea to look over the set-up in 1960 and even before that I had been a Greaves fanatic. At the final whistle I had sprinted over to him and asked him for his jersey which he said he'd give me in the dressing room. As I was shaking hands with other players I heard Jim Baxter ask the same question. Now Greaves knew Baxter better than me but he replied, 'Sorry, I've promised it already.' I really appreciated that. That was also the only time I've gone into the opposition dressing room so keen was I to get that jersey. Alf Ramsey, the England manager, was already there and handing out some stick. He hated being beaten by Scotland and the fact that we inflicted their first defeat as World Champions must have really hurt.

Jimmy Greaves didn't score spectacular goals but they were great goals scored by a special talent. In those early days at Chelsea I had seen him score six goals in two matches. He was good enough to write to me when he was doing his own book to ask me which was the best goal I had scored and my opinion of what I thought was his best goal. He always did the simple thing and the way he operated in the penalty box was sheer magic. If a keeper parried a ball or it came off the woodwork Greaves was there to snap it up and he proved the saying that goalscorers are born and not manufactured. I hit a postwar record for Celtic but to me Greaves will always be the king of goalscorers.

My other hero – Denis Law – was also on the field that day and the fact that we both scored gave me great pleasure. Denis had broken into the Scotland team when I was still at school and I worshipped him. His reflexes and courage were unmatched and his electrifying pace over ten yards gave him a great advantage over defenders.

Earlier in this chapter I referred briefly to Jim Baxter and his arrogance. While it was great to have him on your side I really hated playing against him. When he was with Rangers they dominated in Scotland, and he destroyed Celtic a few times in the early sixties. I remember we were playing abroad when news filtered through that he had been transferred to Sunderland – I was delighted because I knew Rangers would never again be the same power.

We got our revenge on him when we beat Sunderland 5–0 at Roker Park on his debut day but he's a player I'll always remember as one of the real greats. Like so many before him it was a tragedy that his career was so short.

Although Wembley was only my second cap and I had eight more to come the rest were really a bit of an anticlimax.

I played against Russia at Hampden just fifteen days before our European Cup final in 1967. There were six Celts in the side with Willie Wallace adding to the total when he came on as substitute. Big Tam Gemmell lobbed the ball past Ronnie Simpson from about forty yards and that summed up our performance. We just didn't play well that night and to be frank, I thought it was a bad idea to have so many Celtic players in the side for a friendly so soon before Lisbon. The Russians went on to win 2–0 and I'll never know if they were good or we were just plain bad. Certainly it was a great compliment for Celtic to have so many players in the team – but the timing could have been better.

Appearance number four was against Wales in the Home Internationals and although I laid on two crosses which gave Alan Gilzean goals in our 3–2 win at Hampden it was a more important occasion for Jim Craig. It was our right-back's only cap and meant that all of the Lisbon Lions became full internationalists.

I shared a room with Jim before the game and his big fear was the threat of fog. He was worried that his only chance might pass him by. It was special for the club to have everyone capped and other players like John Hughes and Charlie Gallagher – who played for Eire – really swelled the international ranks. I wonder how many teams over the years can boast as many caps at one time.

I played against England at Hampden in 1968 in a 1–1 draw which meant we failed by a point to qualify for the European championship. I had a poor game which stemmed, I think, from using the wrong footwear. Before the match the pitch had been hard and I opted for rubber boots. But heavy rain turned Hampden into a mudbath and I spent most of the afternoon on my rear end.

I recovered from that experience to score our only goal against Denmark in a friendly in Copenhagen and played as substitute – thanks to the British Army – in a World Cup match against Cyprus in Nicosia. With only about fifteen minutes to go a crowd of soldiers began chanting my name and I was promptly sent on and enjoyed a 5–0 win!

An experience in a World Cup match against Austria at Hampden on 6 November 1968 gives me the opportunity of saying how pleased I was that Scotland decided to retain the system of red and yellow cards for referees last year, despite England abolishing them. That night against the Austrians we had won 2–1; I had enjoyed the match because there was a good spirit in the side. But what a shock for Tommy Gemmell and me as we walked from the dressing rooms. A press reporter asked us what we thought about our bookings. We were stunned to say the least. It seemed the referee had cautioned both of us yet he hadn't even spoken to us directly out on the field. Had the card system been in use then at least we would have known that we had to be careful for the remainder of the game – another indiscretion and we could have been ordered off without knowing of a previous booking. My offence had apparently been that I had impeded the goalkeeper. I appeared before the SFA, was told I had no right of appeal and that one more caution would put me out of the next match. So the cards are a good thing for players, spectators and the media. At least with them we know where we stand.

I also played against West Germany before finally hanging up my international boots in a goalless draw against Wales in the Home International championships on 22 April 1970.

It was, I suppose, a fairly short international career compared with that of today's players. But there were fewer matches in those days and a lot of good players pushing for places. Sure I would have liked to have done better and it would have been a thrill to play in a side which reached the World Cup finals. But I've no real regrets. It's been good to see Celtic players like Danny McGrain and Kenny Dalglish win so many caps in the past decade, and they were fortunate to be in the game at a time when Scotland did so well in reaching West Germany in 1974, Argentina in 1978 and Spain in 1982. With many more international matches being played now, the Scotland setup can only get more professional, and that obviously benefits football as a whole in this country. The days of calling for all-tartan teams are over which is also a good thing because in my experience the most patriotic Scots were those playing in English football! The Anglos were always deeply hurt when an all-tartan campaign would start because they were always just as keen to do well. You can't turn your back on a man because he earns his living in England.

If I had one disappointment at Scotland level it was when Jimmy Johnstone got a hard time from the huge Rangers support which followed the international team in those days. They sometimes called for their own favourite, Willie Henderson, and got their way. I know that it was embarrassing for Henderson and a tragedy for Johnstone. Thankfully those days are also in the past – and there to stay I hope. Scotland reached a third successive set of World Cup finals in 1982; such records can only be achieved through a union of fans and players.

To finish this chapter of my playing life here is a list of my full international appearances:

Scotland 2, Northern Ireland 1. Home Internationals, Hampden Park, 16 November 1966. Scorers: Scotland – Murdoch, Lennox; Northern Ireland – Nicholson.

England 2, Scotland 3. Home Internationals, Wembley Stadium, 15 April 1967. Scorers: Scotland – Lennox, Law, McCalliog; England – J. Charlton, Hurst.

Scotland 0, Russia 2. Challenge match, Hampden Park, 10 May 1967. Scorers: Gemmell, o.g., Medvich.

Scotland 3, Wales 2. Home Internationals, Hampden Park, 22 November 1967. Scorers: Scotland – Gilzean 2, McKinnon; Wales – Durban, R. Davies.

Scotland 1, England 1. Home Internationals, Hampden Park, 24 February 1968. Scorers: Scotland – Hughes; England – Peters.

Denmark 0, Scotland 1. Challenge match, Copenhagen, 16 October 1968. Scorer: Lennox.

Scotland 2, Austria 1. World Cup qualifier, Hampden Park, 6 November 1968. Scorers: Scotland – Law, Bremner; Austria – Starek.

Cyprus 0, Scotland 5. World Cup qualifier, Nicosia, 11 December 1968. Scorers: Gilzean (2), Murdoch, Stein (2).

(Lennox sent on as substitute for Stein ten minutes from time.)

Scotland 1, West Germany 1. World Cup qualifier, Hampden Park, 16 April 1969. Scorers: Scotland – Murdoch; West Germany – Muller. (Lennox replaced by Cooke in second half.)

Scotland 0, Wales 0. Home Internationals, Hampden Park, 22 April 1970. Lennox sent on as substitute for McLean in second half. Last appearance in a Scotland jersey. (Ten appearances, three goals.)

European Cup final 1967 — I claim a penalty as Willie Wallace lies on the ground, held round the ankles by Inter Milan goalkeeper Sarti (out of picture)

At the UEFA banquet after winning the European Cup

Six Celts in the Scotland squad gathering in Glasgow, November 1966. *Left to right* McNeill, Gemmell, Murdoch, Clark, Lennox, McBride. Eventually all eleven Lisbon Lions were capped. Fourteen of the sixteen-man first team squad of 1966-7 were international players (including Gallagher, Eire)

Jimmy Johnstone and I training with the Scotland squad

Willie Wallace (7) and Jim Baxter (6) congratulate me after I scored our second goal in the 3-2 win over England at Wembley in 1967 — their first defeat as World Champions

In the 1969 Scottish Cup final we beat Rangers 4-0. Congratulations from Steve Chalmers after I scored the second goal

Jimmy Johnstone and I shared a testimonial match and I was delighted to score the first goal with this header, May 1976

Milan 1970 — we enjoy a laugh at the Varese training headquarters, but the laughs turned to tears in my worst moment in football. *Left to right* Tom Devlin (director), Jim Craig, Jimmy Johnstone, Bobby Lennox, Willie Wallace, Lou Macari, Bertie Auld, Billy McNeill, John Hughes

Jimmy Johnstone and I on an emotional lap of honour after our shared testimonial match. It was his last game for Celtic

# 6

# Milan, 1970

The defeat by the Dutch side Feyenoord in the final of the European Champions' Cup in May 1970 was one of the worst things that ever happened to me in football. It rankles to this day and I doubt whether I'll ever really get over it.

Even the fact that Feyenoord were the best club side I played against in almost twenty years at the top can never compensate for the aftermath of that match in the San Siro Stadium.

San Siro was known as the graveyard of British teams and certainly it never was much of a happy hunting ground for Celtic, although we did manage a couple of draws there. The previous season – 1968–9 – our challenge for the European Cup had ended at the hands of A.C. Milan after a most promising campaign. The fates seemed to dictate during our great days that we cross swords with the Milan clubs or play in their city.

The 1968–9 campaign had begun against St Etienne of France. It was a redrawn tie because Celtic had complained about the Warsaw Pact invasion of Czechoslovakia to UEFA who cancelled our proposed matches against the Hungarian side Ferencvaros. The first leg in St Etienne saw us lose 2–0 and my main memory of the game is of the vast area of the pitch, the biggest playing pitch in Europe; I remember being very tired at full-time. But that didn't stop Jock Stein giving us a rocket. He was far from pleased with our performance and the fact that we had almost lost a third goal in the dying minutes. He had prepared us well for the match and had constantly reminded us that we had been eliminated in the first round the previous year. Obviously we had a big job on hand in the second leg which I missed because of injury. In the event we won 4–0, although the French players were unhappy afterwards with the Czech referee's handling of the game. From our point of view the important factor was that we had survived and it set us up for one of our most memorable nights in the European Cup. We drew the Yugoslav champions, Red Star Belgrade, with the first leg at Celtic Park. At half-time our dressing room was like a mortuary because, despite taking the lead through a fabulous Bobby Murdoch goal early on, the Yugoslavs had equalized before the interval and it was my fault! Sometimes an early goal is the best thing that can happen to a team and sometimes it's the worst thing to happen since it can make you a bit slack in your play. I had been giving chase to one of their players down the left, had thrown myself into a tackle and missed, with the result that Red Star scored.

Big Jock wasn't happy with me and he didn't have to give me reasons. I had been gaining on the player and had I gone on another five yards or so I could have knocked the ball out of play. For an experienced player it was a bad mistake.

But I needn't have worried because in the second half we completely destroyed them thanks to the majestic play of Jimmy Johnstone. He scored two himself and laid on others for Willie Wallace and me. It was one of the greatest, if not the greatest, individual performance ever given at Parkhead and when the fifth goal went in I remember him rushing back to the centre circle shouting, 'I'm no goin', I'm no goin'.' None of us knew what he was on about until afterwards we heard about his deal with Jock Stein. The Wee Man hated flying and had been told he'd be excused the second leg if we won by four goals. Jimmy earned his guarantee that night and, while none of us relished playing an away match without a player of his ability, we understood his problem.

In Belgrade, Red Star were desperate to beat us, but we took the lead when Willie Wallace scored a spectacular forty-yard goal. Although they equalized we were comfortably through to the quarterfinals.

The draw paired us with Italian champions A.C. Milan and the ties captured the imagination of the public in a big way. The first leg was at San Siro (where groundstaff had to paint in red lines because of heavy snow) and we surprised a lot of people by being the first British club to gain a draw in that stadium. At 0–0 we looked forward to the return at Parkhead on 12 March 1969, but four days earlier I was injured against Raith Rovers at Starks Park and missed the game.

For three days I paddled in the Firth of Clyde at Seamill in an attempt to beat the ankle injury, but I failed my fitness test on the morning of the game and that was just the beginning of my disappointments that day. The A.C. Milan striker, Prati, broke away early in the game to score and that was enough to knock us out for another year.

It was a difficult spell for me because of my right ankle. Most days at training I had to put strapping on it, a specialist told me there was 'movement' which shouldn't have been there. He wanted to operate.

But it was at this stage that our chairman Bob Kelly proved again what a wonderful and compassionate man he could be. He told Jock Stein that there was no way he would allow the specialist to cut my ankle, and pointed out that a similar operation had put the Big Man out of football. Mr Kelly's instructions were that I have complete rest from the game and take as much time off as was necessary to get me on the road back to fitness.

As it turned out my season was far from over, and in a way turned out to be one of the most memorable. I recovered in time to take part in a unique experience for the club. Because of a fire at Hampden the previous autumn we had the chance to win the Treble in the space of one month. There had been terrible disappointment for us as we prepared at Seamill for our match against Hibs, and I well remember Jock Stein arriving in the dining

room at breakfast on the Friday morning to tell us the
match had been cancelled. But here we were, months
later, on the threshold of success, and it had all begun with
that League Cup final. My ankle injury seemed a long way
away when I scored a hat trick in our 6–2 win – including
a rare header. We clinched the championship with a draw
against Kilmarnock at Rugby Park.

The most memorable part of the Treble came on 26
April at Hampden Park as we lined up against Rangers in
the Scottish Cup final. We had prepared at Troon without
wingers Jimmy Johnstone and John Hughes, who were
out through injury and suspension. Jock decided to play
George Connelly and Bertie Auld wide with Stevie
Chalmers and me through the middle. It worked perfectly. The full-backs were drawn by the wide men and we
got in behind them. Within sixty seconds I took a corner
out on the left and the minute Billy McNeill connected I
knew it was in the net. I got number two when I ran clear
of the defence to score. It's a difficult type of goal to score
because you know people are snapping at your heels. By
half-time George Connelly had made it three and we were
jubilant in the dressing rooms. But there was always that
nagging suspicion, 'Imagine getting caught.' Any linger-
ing doubts vanished early in the second half when Willie
Henderson missed a chance and Stevie Chalmers got our
fourth to put the icing on the cake.

But in the dying minutes of the game a tackle from
Rangers fullback Willie Mathieson ruined my day. My
ankle was away again and it took me a long time to leave
the field and collect my medal. At least I would have the
close season to recover – or so I thought.

I got through the opening championship and League
Cup games at the start of the 1969–70 season and scored a
few goals in the process. By 25 October we were in another
League Cup final – this time against St Johnstone. I liked
the idea of winning two League Cup medals in six months
but once again my ankle gave way at the vital moment.
We were training at Troon on the Friday and I told Billy
McNeill who offered words of encouragement, 'You'll be

OK, it's a cup final.' But as the day went on I knew there was no chance of playing. I told Neilly Mochan and then went to see Jock Stein. We were always totally honest with each other, and I know he appreciated the fact I didn't try to go into an important game when I was not 100 per cent. Although I lost out on a medal, we knew at Parkhead that we'd reach most cup finals and I consoled myself with the thought that there would be other days of glory. Bertie Auld, who was just back after lengthy injury, scored the only goal of the match, but the joy of winning was tempered by the fact that Stevie Chalmers broke his leg. Bertie's return was to be vital for another European Cup run which would take us all the way to the final.

And before that we had added the Glasgow Cup and were going well in the Scottish Cup to again give us hopes of the grand slam achieved in 1967.

We beat Basle of Switzerland in the opening round on a 2–0 aggregate and learned that they had improved a lot since our previous meeting in 1963. The second round threw us against Portuguese champions Benfica and set us up for a return to Lisbon – scene of our greatest triumph. I missed both legs but the club took me along with Ronnie Simpson and John Clark on a sentimental journey. We visited the Estadio Nacional and generally enjoyed ourselves until the return match itself, when we lost a 3–0 lead in a night of rare drama. The boys did well to survive extra time and then win through on the toss of a coin, although we couldn't help but feel sorry for the Benfica players. It was a most unsatisfactory way to win.

The Italians of Fiorentina stood between us and the quarterfinals but a solid 3–0 win at Parkhead raised our hopes. Bertie Auld got rave notices in the press following the match and I appreciated his coming up to me in the dressing room and telling me how much support I'd given him. That's the type of team we had at Parkhead.

The second leg saw us experience the usual games-manship from the Italians. When we visited the stadium they were obliged under UEFA rules to let us see it under match conditions. But as we stood in total darkness with the damp rising up to our knees they switched on one floodlight pylon, switched it off then switched on another. We saw the ground all right but only a quarter at a time!

My outstanding memory of the trip was Jock Stein's team talk the night before the match. It must have lasted more than an hour and it was brilliant. There was no way we could lose a three-goal lead after it – and we didn't. Fiorentina beat us 1–0 but we were never in any danger.

Jock didn't always give team talks before matches, but when he did they were invariably spot on. One of his favourite ploys on match night was to stand at the mouth of the tunnel as the opposition limbered up before the start. 'Look at him, he's limping,' or, 'He looks a bit cold doesn't he,' would be among his comments as he tried to boost us for kickoff time.

With Fiorentina out of the way we waited for the semifinal draw. I remember a Friday morning after training, we were in the bath when Jock Stein appeared and said simply, 'It's Leeds.'

Jimmy Johnstone immediately quipped, 'Another easy one.' We were certainly getting the most difficult draws in our bid to win the European Cup for the second time.

I remember having butterflies in my stomach when I heard the draw; after all, no one gave us a chance against Don Revie's men. The first leg was at Elland Road and, despite the fact that Jock and Don were the best of pals, there was some psychological warfare used in the build-up. It had been agreed that Leeds would change the colour of their socks for the first leg and we would do likewise in the return, but at the last minute Revie and the referee were insisting that *we* change and we ended up wearing orange socks! They certainly did the trick because we scored right at the start through George Connelly, had another goal disallowed and Wee Jimmy gave their defence a really hot night. A lasting memory of the occasion is the reception we got that night from our supporters – who had travelled there in astonishing numbers. They carried us through the final twenty minutes when Leeds threw everything at us. But we really grafted and chased everything, in the end were worthy of our 1–0 lead.

Despite that victory few people thought we'd make it to the final, and we knew it would still be a mammoth job. Because of the fantastic demand for tickets the second leg was held at Hampden in front of a record crowd for European Cup football – 136,505.

Hampden was never really a noisy place for players, because the crowd was well away from the pitch and the sound travelled upwards. But on the night of 15 April 1970 the blast of noise would have knocked you over. The atmosphere was quite incredible and I'm sure it unnerved some of the Leeds players as they walked out of the tunnel.

Billy Bremner scored first to equalize on aggregate, but goals from John Hughes and Bobby Murdoch saw us through. Bremner was really disappointed afterwards and I remember him telling me that he had been sure they would beat us in Glasgow.

They had played us twice previously in challenge matches at Hampden and Celtic Park without losing and Jackie Charlton, their tall centre-half, had annoyed me when I overheard him say, 'They'll keep bringing us up here till they beat us'. Well we had beaten them in the game that really mattered, and we had a terrific reception as we ran a lap of honour.

But that was to be our last happy night that 1969–70 season. Despite clinching the championship with a draw against Hearts at Tynecastle our dream of the grand slam had finished with a Scottish Cup final defeat at the hands of Aberdeen in controversial circumstances.

Referee Bobby Davidson had given them an early penalty, which baffled everyone at Hampden, then denied us one after Martin Buchan had almost halved me in two! He then disallowed a goal after Aberdeen's keeper Bobby Clark had dropped the ball at my feet in the first half. Mr Davidson was well behind the play and couldn't possibly have seen what had happened. I can only believe to this day that he made his decision as a result of controversy between Clark and me in the previous season when I had scored in similar circumstances at Parkhead. Bobby Clark had come out in the newspapers accusing me of knocking the ball out of his hands.

Even when the Dons were 2–0 up I felt we could catch them, and I did get one back. But they scored again to make it 3–1 and there was then no way we could repeat our success of 1967.

But the greatest prize of them all still awaited us – the European Cup. It was to be the pinnacle of five years of tremendous successes for the club, and the final proof to English critics that our win in Lisbon had been no flash in the pan.

But right from the word go things started to go wrong. The night before we left our training headquarters at Troon, manager Jock Stein informed us that Milan was badly hit by strikes and that the match might be switched to Rome. It was hardly the ideal start for such an important match.

Our training headquarters at Varese, where we had stayed before, were very monastic and lacked the atmosphere of our HQ of Estoril in 1967. There the fans would come along and give you a sense of occasion, but Varese was well out of their reach.

A lot has been said and written about Milan in the past decade or so, but as far as I'm concerned I feel we prepared thoroughly for the match. We talked about Feyenoord's strengths and weaknesses and our training was brisk.

On the evening of 6 May we were preparing to leave on the eighty-minute journey when I had a strange encounter with Jock Stein. As my room-mate Jimmy Johnstone was getting dressed I wandered onto the balcony looking out over rolling hills and forest. It was a peaceful setting. I was singing a song, probably trying to settle the nerves, when I heard a voice say, 'It must be great to be a player and have no problems'. I looked down to my right and there on a balcony below was Jock Stein.

'What problems?' I asked.

He replied, 'The pressures are always on the manager'.

It brought home to me the loneliness of being a manager. Once we were over that white line there wasn't much he could do except hope we'd play well.

We left early that evening in case of traffic problems but it rebounded on us. I found I was stripped and ready to play far too early, and that's a bad thing for any player. When you hang about a dressing room too long the nerves start to jangle. Another bad thing that night was when we went out to inspect the pitch and were met by the blast of the Dutch horns. It was a totally foreign sound which drowned out our fans and created a horrible atmosphere. Everything felt wrong and I remember lining up before kickoff time and noticing the smart tracksuit gear worn by the Dutch. We were former European champions, but they had much better gear than us.

We scored an early goal but I knew we were struggling. When I got the ball I felt totally isolated; they buzzed all over the park, they were the best team I've ever played against. They could have beaten us by five or six goals that night; they hit woodwork several times and created a barrowload of chances. We lost a bad goal to them in the first half and never really recovered. Billy McNeill headed the ball as it was going out of play. Our goalkeeper Evan Williams said afterwards that he had shouted to him to let it go but amidst the din of those horns it was impossible to hear anything. The match, amazingly, went to extra time and John Hughes almost gave us the lead. We had thought Feyenoord would tire in the extra period but they didn't and got the winner just four minutes from time. We pushed forward to try and save the game and I remember being left in a crazy situation when they broke upfield. I was left to chase one of their players and as I tackled I hit the ball against my own crossbar. That would have been the final irony.

The final whistle was a nightmare. Our players were weeping openly. I watched the Feyenoord players raise the magnificent silver trophy high into the air – a trophy

I had once held. Its gold lining shimmered under the floodlights and how I envied them their lap of honour – something we had been denied.

I have no recollection of receiving my runner-up medal and I can't remember much until the journey back to the hotel. Our wives had joined us on the team bus but no one spoke a word for about twenty minutes and even then we didn't know what to say. We looked like the survivors of an atomic war. Jimmy Johnstone and Jim Brogan could hardly walk – even had we managed to hold out for a replay we would have been struggling to field a team. We all felt absolutely sick when we arrived back at Varese. Sure we had been confident before the match, if you're not confident then you've no chance in football, but we certainly hadn't been over confident. Later there was a lot of speculation about whether or not we had been more interested in making money or playing football. It was true that we had appointed an agent, but that had been with an eye to the following season.

The only victory of Milan was won by our fans. Despite delays at the airport the following day their behaviour was magnificent in trying circumstances. When they could have had a go at us, they did just the opposite, they gave us their support and that made us feel a lot better. But it took me a long time to get Milan out of my system, I don't think the memory of that deep disappointment will ever go away.

And it didn't help having to leave for an American tour just a few days after returning home from Italy. We kept thinking what are we doing here? We were supposed to have the European Cup with us, instead we were empty-handed. The games in America were disastrous as well. We lost to Manchester United and then had two matches against an Italian side, Bari – one of the worst sides I ever met.

After the first meeting with Bari one of their players told me that I was for the chop – and he got me in the second meeting, which ended in total farce. They were reduced to nine men and, with the game at 2–2, we were awarded a penalty kick. The Italians promptly walked off the field. We stood about for a while and a committee from the organizers emerged to tell us that Bari would return if we agreed to miss the penalty! Bobby Murdoch, who was standing over the ball, said that he intended to put it in the roof of the net.

There were a few dollars at stake for the players, and the Italians eventually agreed to come back on and face the music, but after a further delay the committee returned to tell us that the referee had left the ground in a taxi some twenty minutes earlier. The penalty was never taken, the match was abandoned and the players' dollars withheld! 1970 was not our year.

# 7

# New Faces

Four years to the very month after we had become the first British team to win the European Champions' Cup, the Lisbon Lions made their very last appearance amidst great publicity. The date was 1 May 1971, the venue Celtic Park. It was a league match against Clyde, sandwiched between our having clinched the championship for the sixth time in a row and a Scottish Cup final against Rangers which was to bring another victory.

Our manager Jock Stein, always a man with a touch of showmanship, hit on the idea of a grand finale for his favourite sons, and packed the ground for what otherwise would have been a fairly meaningless match.

I have several memories of that marvellous afternoon, including the fact that the main stand was under major reconstruction and the roof had been removed. It meant that we had to walk through the old enclosure onto the field. The Jungle and the terraces were overflowing with fans there for a day of unashamed nostalgia – and that's what they got.

We overwhelmed Clyde by 6–1 with a vintage performance. I thought the team operated as well that day as it had ever done – even allowing for the fact that the league was over as a contest. The only change came in goal, where Evan Williams took over, but the great Ronnie Simpson was there to take part in the pre-match kickabout before going off to a great cheer in what turned out to be a tremendous occasion. After a couple of early goals with Bertie Auld, Bobby Murdoch and Jimmy

Johnstone in the side you knew you were home and dry, and I was delighted at scoring a hat trick.

We were like a well-oiled machine; all the parts were there and working smoothly. The one sadness of the day was that Bertie Auld was making his final appearance for the club, but he turned it into a great personal triumph. At one stage I heard a roar as we moved forward, I turned around to see Bertie walking in the opposite direction with a raised arm, clenched fist and that impish grin in evidence as the entire Jungle rose to him. It brought a lump to my throat and the punters were obviously loving every moment of it. At the end of the game the players rushed up to him, raised him shoulder high and carried him from the field in a very emotional departure. A few of the lads were really upset that day – and none more than me.

Bertie Auld was a player who had a lot of influence on my own career. I remember him making his first appearance after returning from Birmingham, the date was 16 January 1965 – a cold, wintry day and the team lost by 2–1 to Hearts at Parkhead. Bertie, though, showed that he had gained a lot of experience in the south and the following week when I got back into the team he provided a cross from the left which let me score with a rather vital header in a 3–3 draw with Morton at Cappielow. It was to be the beginning of a partnership which would bring many a goal for Celtic over the next six years.

Bertie was a marvellous passer of the ball and could place it perfectly for me when I started a run. We in fact had three great passers in that era: Bobby Murdoch and Charlie Gallagher were as good as any in that department. I just had to make a move and they provided the perfect service. Had the ball still been of the laced variety, they could have guided it to you with the lace away from either your head or your boot.

Later, Harry Hood proved to be very good in that way. Harry in fact was one of the players who had come into the side in season 1968–9 after his transfer from Clyde and he was joined by Tom Callaghan from Dunfermline Athletic.

The following season youngsters like Vic Davidson and Lou Macari began knocking on the door with a few first-team appearances and it was obvious that a challenge now faced the Lisbon Lions.

That led to false accusations at the time that Jock Stein had broken up the European Cup winning side too early. There's no doubt Big Jock was proud of that team. He loved the side, and in fact he had said immediately after Lisbon that it was a team which would never be beaten. Some people took that as a hint that it would never play together again. In actual fact it played very few games after that – and never again in any type of cup final. There was always a small change here or there and even when we played Real Madrid in the di Stefano testimonial match just a couple of weeks after Lisbon he played John Fallon and Willie O'Neill. He was shrewd was Big Jock! He was obviously faced in 1970–1 with the dilemma of choosing between young players who were breaking through at a great rate and his loyalty to those who had achieved so much for him. But he had to balance things for the good of the club and I believe he did it in the right way.

At one stage we had two teams which could well have won the championship. The established players were well aware of the challenge ahead; you only had to see Kenny Dalglish in action to see he wasn't far off perfection. If you gave him the ball in training he just steadied himself and put it in the net with consummate ease.

On top of that there was Lou Macari, George Connelly, David Hay, Danny McGrain and Vic Davidson – it was easy to see why they called themselves the 'Quality-Street Kids'.

These players were certainly edging their way into the side, which knocks on the head the theory that Jock Stein was breaking things up. If you don't give youth its fling, then it's obvious the younger players will be looking to other pastures. And anyway, how many times does a team win a trophy and go on as the same unit to retain it the following season? Football, like all other aspects of life, is a continually changing process. Just get out a Celtic team picture from even a couple of seasons ago and you'll agree with me.

And who's to say if the Lisbon Lions had played on at every opportunity that the club would have gone on to record nine consecutive championships plus all the other honours in that period. Players must have a challenge and that is exactly what was happening in the late sixties and early seventies.

Surely the proof that the changes were gradual rather than forced comes when you look at the team which played in the 1970 European Cup final against Feyenoord in Milan. Ronnie Simpson's career was over because of injury, David Hay had, through his own high standards, made the right-back position his own. Jim Brogan had taken over from John Clark while John Hughes – a member of the first-team squad for a decade – had replaced Steve Chalmers who was recovering from a broken leg. People tend to think of the Lisbon Lions as eleven players. But it's worth remembering that we travelled to Lisbon with no fewer than fourteen inter-national players in our ranks. Players like Hughes, Charlie Gallagher and Willie O'Neill had all played at some stage in the campaign and had made big con-tributions.

The post-Milan period was not only one of great change but also terrible tragedy in the form of the Ibrox disaster on 2 January 1971 when sixty-six people lost their lives. Yet we players were unaware of the situation until a good while after we had left the ground that day.

It had been a typical Old Firm game, and we were in the closing minute when I tried a shot from twenty-five yards – something I seldom did. This time I had connected well and the ball came crashing down off the crossbar allowing Jimmy Johnstone to score. I was sure we had won but the game went on and, just seconds later, Rangers got a free kick and the ball was suddenly in our net. The whistle sounded and we left the field tied at 1–1.

All I remembered afterwards was the length of time we waited for our bus to pull away. It was certainly a good bit longer than usual. Then just as we left someone said there had been an accident and a couple of supporters had been killed. That was bad enough. But by the time we arrived back at Celtic Park to pick up our cars we heard the death toll might be as high as twelve. On the way home to Saltcoats I heard more news on the car radio and gradually the full horror unfolded. All I could think was that we had been fortunate to have missed the harrowing scenes which took place at Ibrox that evening as dressing rooms and corridors were turned into a temporary mortuary It was without doubt a chapter of terrible grief in the history of the game in this country.

The following season – 1971–2 – I scored my 200th competitive goal for Celtic against Airdrie at Broomfield. Willie Wallace provided a cross from the left at the top end of the ground and it was a pretty special personal moment for me. Another goal I treasured that season was one at Aberdeen on 11 March 1972, which was a giant step towards beating off the Dons' strong challenge and clinching our seventh consecutive title.

My goals total that season was nineteen but the pressure was certainly on from the Quality-Street Kids and, to add to Bertie Auld's departure from the previous season, came the transfers of John Hughes and Willie Wallace to Crystal Palace and Tommy Gemmell to Nottingham Forest.

Season 1972–3 saw me hold my own against the rising tide of youth, with seventeen goals – although my number of first-team appearances began to drop a bit.

But I was never the type to look over my shoulder and worry. I believed if you were good enough and kept producing the goals then you would get a chance. If not . . . tough luck.

It was a mixed season for us. For the third year running we had battled our way to the League Cup final and for the third time lost – this time to Hibs. Then in the Scottish Cup final there was further disappointment. It was the centenary final and attended for the first time by a member of the Royal Family – Princess Alexandra. I could only get a place on the bench that day but I remember my first touch of the ball when I replaced the injured Jim Brogan after sixty minutes – I had to kick off after Rangers took the lead! While I had been waiting to get onto the field Rangers had surged forward and won a free kick. Then as I jogged onto the park I saw Tommy McLean float the ball towards Derek Johnstone. His header came off a post and Tom Forsyth forced the ball over the line. Rangers held on to win 3–2 in front of a crowd of 122,714 to complete an unhappy cup season for us.

But in the championship itself we were still top dogs and went on to clinch our eighth consecutive title in a tremendous afternoon at Easter Road. People ask which was the most satisfying of those championship wins. The truth is they were all special because we had to battle hard wherever we went. It's often said that the Premier Division is much more competitive than the old setup, I wouldn't argue against that having played in both competitions. But let no one ever underestimate the challenges that faced us in our great run. We had to go to places like Dunfermline and Kilmarnock where in those days you got a really hard match. It was never easy and I remember some hair-raising moments in those title wins. If people had seen how drained we were in the dressing room after these games they would have known just how tough it was.

The great thing about us then – and I make no apology for repeating myself – is that as a team we were true professionals. No matter who the opposition was we treated them with the utmost respect.

I think what we did do – which many teams including Celtic sides have failed to do since – was that once we had a team on the run we would, in the true tradition of a good boxer, finish them off. How often do you see teams these days get a goal ahead, play the opposition off the park yet suddenly get caught against the run of play.

Season 1973–4 saw us clinch our ninth straight championship and complete the double yet again by taking the Scottish Cup with a fine 3–0 win over Dundee United. Our greatest disappointment that season came in the European Cup when we can genuinely say we were 'robbed' in two infamous matches with the Spaniards of Atletico Madrid, which I'll talk about later in this chapter.

First of all I would like to concentrate on a very special moment for me that year. I scored twenty-one goals – twelve championship, two Scottish Cup, six League Cup and one European Cup. Those scores helped me to break Steve Chalmers' record of 241 goals. Steve had held the postwar record which had made him second only to the legendary Jimmy McGrory in the scoring stakes at Parkhead. So it was a great feeling to move into second spot – and it goes to show what success Celtic achieved in the sixties and seventies when two players from the same era filled second and third place in the club's goalscoring history.

It also makes you think about what a player Jimmy McGrory must have been. He hit 550 goals in first class football – a British record which stands to this day and is unlikely ever to be beaten. Five hundred and fifty! It's mind boggling. He must have counted the ones he got in training! I only knew Jimmy McGrory as a manager – the man who signed me for Celtic – and by that time he was a gentle, pipe-smoking man in his mid-fifties. As a youngster he must have been a one-man army and it's worth pointing out that with 410 league goals in 408 matches he's the only player ever in these islands to average just over a goal a game. Jimmy McGrory obviously deserves the very special place he holds in the unique story of a great club.

According to our club records I actually equalled Steve Chalmers' record on 17 November 1973 with a goal against Partick Thistle at Parkhead, although you could say I was slightly upstaged that afternoon by a man called John 'Dixie' Deans who hit six past Scotland keeper Alan Rough for a postwar record in a single match. Watching rather uncomfortably from the stand that day was Jimmy McGrory who had hit the all-time record of eight against Dunfermline way back in the twenties. We're quite a club for setting the pace!

I overtook Steve's record the following week when I scored with a penalty in a 2–0 win over Dumbarton at Boghead. And seconds later I was substituted. How's that for celebrating a triumphant moment! But at the end of the game Kenny Dalglish who got our other goal that day, led the boys into the dressing room to congratulate me.

I mentioned earlier our exit from the European Cup at the hands of Atletico Madrid and this was quite a disappointment in my career. To get into the Champions' Cup you have to sweat blood to win your own league. So you never take it lightly when you go out – especially in the circumstances of the 1973–4 campaign when we had performed really well to reach the semifinals for the fourth time in seven years – a marvellous record. I didn't play in the first leg at Parkhead but watched from the stand as the Spaniards stooped to every shady tactic in the book. They had two players ordered off and others booked in probably the worst show of bad behaviour ever witnessed at Celtic Park. In fact one more ordering off would have seen the game abandoned. Jimmy Johnstone showed tremendous courage that night as he was constantly hacked to the ground. But he kept carrying the game to Atletico who amazingly held out and got a 0–0 draw. Our players were positive that they would not be required to travel to Spain for the return leg. It was generally thought that the Spaniards would be kicked out of the tournament by UEFA and at the very worst we would have to face them on neutral soil.

Then one night, midway between the European dates, we were in Dunfermline and having a pre-match meal when Jock Stein called everyone together and announced, 'The news is that we're playing Atletico Madrid in Madrid.' We all looked at each other in disbelief. He added, 'That's it, we have to play them there so forget about it for now. I want you thinking only of tonight's match.'

The following week we took off from Glasgow airport and within minutes the war of nerves had started. The club had chartered an Aer Lingus plane and the Spaniards instructed the pilot that an Irish airliner must fly out of its home base. So we were diverted to Dublin where we touched down, opened a door to take aboard the morning papers as proof that we'd been there and roared off along the runway again in the direction of Madrid. Jimmy Johnstone was not amused, yet his troubles, unknown to him, were merely beginning. On arrival at Madrid we got the first real hint of what was to come. Armed guards in trucks met us, surrounded our bus and guided us to our hotel where they took up positions around the swimming pool and the roof. It appeared the whole of Spain had it in for us – certainly that's the message we were getting. There had been an incredible anti-Celtic campaign in part of the media; we felt not too popular.

As usual I was sharing a room with Jimmy Johnstone and the first night there the phone rang. The Wee Man answered and a voice in broken English informed him, 'Johnstone, you are a dead man.' That was followed swiftly by rumours that a sniper would lie in wait for him. That was enough for Jimmy. He ordered me to shut the blinds in our room and we lived that way for the next few days.

At one point he lifted an orange and in an effort to lessen the tension I joked that possibly a syringe had been used to poison it. But that effort backfired and he had the fruit bowl removed from the room. Naturally he was worried, but to be honest it never really bothered me. Let's face it, the sniper would have to have been a bad shot to miss him and hit me!

Jock Stein also tried to calm him by saying that he too had been threatened. He told the Wee Man, 'At least you can jink about on the park – I'm a sitting duck in that dugout.' Jock left it to Jimmy to make up his own mind about taking part in the match and he decided to play.

We set out for the stadium with army trucks and police outriders, armed to the teeth, all around us. When we arrived we were deposited behind a special fence to keep the jeering, spitting Spaniards away from us – and this was about two hours before kickoff time! Gerry McNee has told me that at the pre-match press conference he attended the Atletico officials threw a champagne reception for the media, handed out little gifts and said in a statement, 'We cannot understand what happened in Glasgow. That is in the past and now we just want to play good football.' That was easy now that they had home advantage and 80,000 people on their side.

Before getting stripped for the match we went onto the field for the usual inspection and got such a hostile reception we had to head back to the dressing rooms again. It was incredible. Even during half-time the whistling and jeering never let up and our substitutes had to abandon their warm-up in case of sparking off a riot. They had been whipped up into some kind of nationalistic frenzy. Even Juan Carlos, now King of Spain, was there to cheer on his boys. It was a match – despite everything – that we could have won. We missed chances before they scored late in the game. I remember, for instance, Kenny Dalglish having an uncharacteristic miss in front of goal but you can never blame one person or one missed chance in a game like that. I remember, too, Denis Connaghan having a good match for us in goal. But we were really never meant to win that one and, on reflection, had we been victors I think we could have experienced difficulties in getting away from the stadium.

Once again we had come to grief against a team with a strong Argentinian make-up – including their manager Lorenzo. They really were hatchet men, and yet you were always left wondering why they play like that. They have so much talent but they resort to the worst tactics in football. I think it's fair to say that justice was done when Bayern Munich beat them 4–0 in the final replay a short time later. Victory for the Spaniards that year would have set football back a long time.

As I said earlier, the season finished well with our ninth consecutive championship win, and we hit one more high note when we took the Scottish Cup down to Anfield for the Ron Yeats testimonial match. We paraded the cup to the Kop then beat their heroes 4–1. The great Bobby Charlton was Celtic's guest that night and I was glad to lay on the opening goal for him. Afterwards I was very flattered by comments he made on television about my performance when he said, 'Bobby Lennox should never be out of the Scotland squad.' Coming from a man of his stature in the game it was a compliment indeed.

The following season, 1974–5, was to be a traumatic one for Celtic on several fronts. On a personal note I scored only seven goals and I had further disappointment when I was sent off in the European Cup against the Greek team Olympiakos in Athens. It was the second ordering off of my career and almost as big a farce as Montevideo. We had drawn the first-round, first-leg tie 1–1 at Celtic Park in a disappointing match. The return was to be much worse as we went down 2–0. It was a typical atmosphere for a Greek stadium with firecrackers going off all over the place. I had come on as a substitute and a short time later came my first brush with the referee. The Greeks were awarded a free kick and with one of their danger men about to take it I stood in front of the ball to give our defence time to get organized. Meanwhile Olympiakos officials indicated they wanted to make a substitution. I was busy watching the linesman flagging to get the referee's attention. But the ref. was having none of it. He wanted the free kick taken and suddenly he came running over, pulled me away from the ball and showed me the yellow card. I couldn't believe it and neither could the Greek striker who just burst out laughing and began shrugging his shoulders.

Then a few minutes later I went into a tackle and blocked the ball only for a Greek player to fly over my shoulder and let out the most horrendous scream. I looked across the park and the man in black was racing towards me with the red card in his hand. All our lads just stood and shook their heads. But Jock Stein wasn't so sympathetic. He gave me a bawling out afterwards not for being ordered off but for not using my experience in backing away from the ball at the first incident. The years I had been in the game should have taught me not to drop my guard for a moment.

Yet referees in these European ties interpret rules and do things very differently from those in the game at home. There seem to be so many misunderstandings in European matches. Whether it's caused by the atmosphere and the tension I just don't know. But I saw the same thing happen to Bobby Murdoch in Russia in late 1967. Jim Craig had made a good, clean tackle but was penalized. Murdoch bounced the ball off the ground in frustration and was immediately sent packing. Again experience should have taught him not to get involved, yet how can such an action be deemed an ordering-off offence? In Europe you have to tread a tightrope . . . walk on tip-toes because anything can and does happen. British teams seem to have the stiff upper-lip approach. Sure they'll go in with the hard tackle and whack an opponent. But many foreign teams adopt the sneaky approach. They'll spit and use the elbows. They pull jerseys and generally go out of their way to distract you from the job in hand and there can be no doubt that at times the European scene is devalued because of this attitude.

On the domestic front in 1974–5 we ended a bad run of League Cup final defeats by demolishing Hibs 6–3 and again won the Scottish Cup with a 3–1 win over Airdrie. But our great run of nine championships in a row came to an end when Rangers won the league for the first time in eleven years.

There were further shocks too. Minutes after the Scottish Cup final Billy McNeill announced his retirement from the game and there were more transfers. Jim Brogan was given a free as was my buddy Jimmy Johnstone who just a year earlier had been in the World Cup squad.

When I heard the news about the Wee Man my mind

went back to a chilling comment from Jock Stein at the end of the previous season when he stated in the club's *Celtic View* summer magazine:

'Then there's Jimmy Johnstone. What can I say about him? He's an enigma. In the shadows for so much of the season he suddenly takes a tumble to himself and there's all the old artistry and ball skills in full flower. So much so that he finds himself back in Scotland's colours and a Hampden hero in the win against England. However, Johnstone will have to show more dedication if he is to be any use to Celtic next season.'

The departure of Jimmy and Billy meant that quite suddenly I was the last of the Lisbon Lions. But despite all the comings and goings I never thought, It must be my turn next.

In fact I was far from being finished and just about to gain one of the great honours of my career.

During the close season the club had been thrown into turmoil by the news that Jock Stein had been very badly injured in a car crash and it was touch and go for a while whether or not he would pull through. We had just lost our captain through retirement and so many big names had departed the club as the youngsters broke through.

But footballers get on with their jobs no matter what's going on in the background and we trained hard in readiness for a season which we all knew would be a tough one for us.

Then one day just before season 1975–6 Sean Fallon, who had been appointed interim manager, said after training that Jock Stein would announce the new club captain on his return but meantime Bobby Lennox would carry out that role. What a thrill that was for me after so many years at Parkhead, and what made it all the more enjoyable was the fact that a huge cheer went up in the dressing room. I was as pleased as punch when I led the lads onto the field and negotiated for them behind the scenes until eventually Kenny Dalglish took over as skipper.

It had always been on the cards that Kenny would get

the job and such a brilliant player deserved it. But as I said, I felt it was a great honour to hold the post, even for such a short time.

I managed only thirteen goals that season and it turned out to be the first since season 1963–4 that we had failed to win any of the major trophies.

However Jock Stein was on the mend again, and he took charge of his first match for more than a year the night of my joint testimonial with Jimmy Johnstone. Suddenly the trying months were behind us and a night of great emotion in store.

# 8

# Jimmy and Me

It was just after 9.40 p.m. on the night of 17 May 1976 when Jimmy Johnstone and I ran together for the last time as Celtic team-mates. Yet the natural sadness was pushed into the background because of the 50,000 fans who had refused to go home, and insisted on giving us the sort of acclaim the Romans gave their victorious gladiators. It was a magical moment for me.

Jimmy, in fact, had broken the news to me that a committee had approached the club with a view to giving us a joint testimonial match against Manchester United and that Celtic had agreed. To be honest I was surprised in two ways. It had never entered my head that I was due a testimonial because other members of the Lisbon team like Bertie Auld and Bobby Murdoch had been allowed to leave and fix their own terms with other clubs. It was also a bit of a shock, in that I still had a year of my contract to run and it crossed my mind that perhaps Celtic were telling me it was time to say goodbye. But retirement was certainly not in my immediate plans. Jimmy, of course, had left Celtic the previous year.

The only Celtic player in modern times to receive a testimonial had been Billy McNeill who was always a big hero of mine. He had been there when I had signed and had been my captain through everything we achieved during the great years. He certainly deserved his.

Some people commented in 1976 that Jimmy and I should have had a testimonial each. Certainly in terms of finance we would have been better off. But neither of us could complain about the cheques we took away that night. And it was apt that we should be together on that special Monday in May, we had been through thick and thin together.

On the afternoon of the match we had met at a restaurant in Glasgow, and I remember the fury on the Wee Man's face as he walked in the door. It matched the thunder clouds above the city.

The committee had sensibly decided against an all-ticket match because of the inconvenience to fans having to make a double journey. But that afternoon the decision was unpopular. It had been raining cats and dogs since the early morning. 'Look at it,' said Jimmy, 'we'll be lucky if we get 10,000. I wouldn't go to a game in this weather.' Once again I had to try and use any soothing influence I had, although I must admit I had a few doubts myself.

I remember saying, 'People will come out to see Jimmy Johnstone. No danger. We'll get a good crowd tonight.' By the time we got into the taxi the rain had eased and Jimmy reckoned we would get 15,000, so at least his mood was improving. I was never a betting man but I put up a fiver that we would draw 30,000 to 35,000. As it turned out the crowd was an unbelievable 50,000.

Yet when we arrived at the ground it was still fairly quiet though we were soon cheered up by comedian Billy Connolly who was there to referee a bounce game before the main event. The dressing rooms were bedlam with players and ex-players milling about and before we knew where we were kickoff time was approaching. One thing which had me laughing was when Nobby Stiles, Manchester United's likeable hard-man, came in looking for a pair of boots. I helped him out and he thanked me in courteous manner. A few minutes later he was in again, and I asked him if they fitted. He was only a few yards away as he screwed up his eyes trying to figure out who I was, he couldn't see a thing without his specs! I also remember the great Bobby Charlton coming in and paying both Jimmy and me a handsome tribute.

Next thing there was a knock on the door and it was time to go out. Billy Connolly told us the place was mobbed and the Wee Man quipped: 'I hope it's a late kickoff.' Our chairman, Desmond White, and Manchester United's Matt Busby led the way from the tunnel with Jimmy and I walking behind them and followed by the teams. The roar was incredible, as loud as it had been at any of our great home matches in the European Cup and for the entire match the crowd seemed to chant our names non-stop. Davie Hay had returned from Chelsea for the night to play in the green-and-white hoops and he also got a wonderful reception – as did all the boys.

David, in fact, laid on the opening goal with a great cross which I headed into the net – that goal meant as much as any of the 300 or so I scored for Celtic. The match had been billed with Jimmy as the most exciting winger in Europe, the man who could take people on and entertain, and I was billed as the man who could score goals. To have done my job once again in front of that loyal crowd meant everything to me. And the Wee Man was brilliant throughout the game, going on those jinking runs which had torn the very soul out of so many top teams. Kenny Dalglish also had a brilliant evening scoring a hat trick which included a fabulous chip shot over the United keeper. We won 4–0 and I remember them pulling off players and replacing them with fresh legs because we were in such energetic form.

At the final whistle we walked to the side of the pitch and Jimmy Nicholl came running over and asked for my jersey. I asked him to hold on and that I'd gladly give him it in the dressing room. But he was persistent. 'If you go on a lap of honour they'll grab it off you,' he said. By this time I was rather flattered and could hardly say no, so that's why the Wee Man and I set off round the track with him wearing a Celtic shirt and me in the colours of Manchester United.

As long as I live I'll remember the scenes as we ran past the stand towards the Springfield Road end of the ground and then past the Jungle to the other terracing. Hundreds of scarves were thrown at our feet and thousands more were held aloft in what looked like lines of unbroken chains around the entire stadium. When we arrived back at the tunnel Jock Stein said, 'You'll have to go round again. They've no intention of going home.' By this time our legs were weary and we decided to go into the centre of the field. Then Jimmy headed back towards the Jungle, always his favourite part of the ground. The crowd in there worshipped the Wee Man. He took off his boots and in a final gesture threw them into the fans who had watched him for the last time. I got caught up in that scene and was just about to do the same when I had to stop in my tracks. It suddenly struck me that we were playing a game at Portsmouth a few nights later and these were the only boots I possessed which were broken in. So in case anyone thought I was a bit mean that night – that was the reason!

As we walked back across the park for the last time, arms round one another's shoulders, not much was said although I remember the Wee Man's words, 'That's me away and you're still here. You don't know how lucky you are.' It was a sad moment and what made it worse was the fact that Jimmy Johnstone should have had many more years in Celtic's colours. It was nothing short of tragic and he's the first to admit that himself.

I believe that if Jimmy had lived in a place like Saltcoats he would have enjoyed a longer career. In Uddingston he was too near the city and too easily led. More than once he said to me 'If you hadn't left when you did last night I'd probably have stayed on.' Not that he was up to anything wrong, simply that he would be tempted to stay out late. I'm not saying I'm the greatest guy in the world when it comes to calling it a night but we got on well together and I think I had some influence over him.

People often asked me how I rated Jimmy among all the players I met in my career. My simple answer is that I rate him the tops. Who could you compare him with? In the autumn of his career there was talk of him dropping back into midfield but he would never have had to do that.

Jimmy was always capable of playing wide because he was still sharp. He could make a yard for himself even against faster players.

How did our relationship begin? Well, we shared a lot of interests, we had a similar sense of humour, liked the Beatles and could enjoy a good laugh. We were the ones who started the singsongs. Like Billy McNeill and John Clark or Bertie Auld and Tommy Gemmell, we would share a room on trips and that went all the way back to our great American trip of 1966.

In those early days Jimmy was a great trainer. He'd be up front driving himself on. In fact all of the players then worked very hard. If they enjoyed themselves the previous night then they made up for it the next day on the track. The standard of our fitness was brought home to me recently by Jim Lumsden, our youth coach at Parkhead. He had been at Roker Park in 1965 and had witnessed us playing a seven-a-side match for fifteen minutes on the full pitch. He remembered some other players from the south laughing at us and asking, 'Are they professionals? They'll never last a game after that.' Yet they got their answer when we beat Sunderland – Jim Baxter and all – by 5–0!

As I said, Jimmy was a great trainer but it was also evident that he had worked immensely hard on his skills as a youngster. I remember him telling me that when he was a boy he had bought the Stanley Matthews book on football skills and had practised ball control, running in and out past milk bottles and anything else he could find. Even people with natural ability have to work to improve, and he did. What people saw on a Saturday was something special but what we, the players, saw him do in training was incredible. There's no doubt the players saw the best of him. He could pull the ball down and beat three men at close quarters, yet we never felt the slightest resentment if he made a monkey out of us. He'd come at you with the ball and jink past you. I always knew which way he was going but he'd simply drop his shoulder and send you the wrong way. All you could do was fall on your back and laugh. On the odd occasion when you picked the right way he could lift the ball over your foot, and he was really sharp at getting away from a tackle. And if he was in a side leading by a few goals at training he'd double back and do the same to you again! But he was never the sort of player who would set out in a match to humiliate an opponent or make a fool of him. And that was a characteristic of the entire side. We would go out and win 6–0 rather than win 2–0 and waste time taking the mickey.

I've often been asked what was Jimmy's greatest game and really it's difficult to pick one when I witnessed so many at such close quarters. I remember him playing a stormer of a league match against Dundee United at Parkhead where he was the inspiration behind seven goals. I was a spectator that night and got a different view again of his genius. Then there was the famous Red Star match mentioned in an earlier chapter. A lasting memory of him comes from the Bernabeu Stadium the night we played in the di Stefano benefit match. He dropped that shoulder again and bewildered a defender to such an extent that even the partisan crowd had to rise to its feet and cheer. He also had a fabulous game in the 1971 Scottish Cup final replay against Rangers, which some people called Johnstone's final.

There were so many great days and nights involving the Wee Man and one of the good things about having him as a team-mate was the comforting thought that in a crisis you need only give him the ball and he would keep it for a while and take the pressure off you. It's often been said that at times he wasn't content to make the ball talk but liked to make it sing occasionally as well!

Jimmy and controversy often walked hand in hand and there's no denying that he could be temperamental. I vividly remember in the early sixties Bobby Murdoch having a much-publicized go at him on the park in a match against Partick Thistle. Bobby had hit a pass inside a defender which Jimmy hadn't bothered to chase. He liked the ball at his feet. And being the darling of the fans it was poor Bobby who got a roasting from the terraces.

Then there was Jimmy's sometimes tempestuous relationship with Jock Stein. They had their differences over the years, although it's an undeniable fact that they had a deep respect for each other's ability: to Jimmy, Jock's word was law and he would play to instruction. One of their most celebrated fall-outs came during a match at Parkhead in which the Big Man substituted the Wee Man. Jimmy gestured towards the dugout and began taking off his jersey on the way to the tunnel.

He told me afterwards that he almost died when he got to the dressing room and heard the thunder of the manager's feet behind him. But that was Jimmy, within seconds of doing something like that he'd be full of remorse.

Jimmy loved going to Seamill, just a couple of miles along the Ayrshire coast from my own home. Long walks, fresh air, a good book and an early night really relaxed him. I was never out with him in Glasgow except at functions connected with the club. Even though we were close we didn't socialize away from Celtic Park and I never envied him city life.

But at the quiet of Seamill it came across to me that he envied my way of life. He would say things like, 'You're a lucky man, you've got great lungs.' You'd have thought he was a doctor! He would go on about the advantages I had as a child being able to swim and run on the beach. Seamill brought out the best in him. He would go on a real health kick, and even arrive with a bottle of Lucozade. In the evenings we would sit in the lounge and listen to Jock Stein talking about the old stories before our own playing days. I always loved Seamill and still do. I seldom played a bad game after a few days there.

Another legend surrounding Jimmy was his fear of flying, which certainly did haunt him for a good while. It all began when he returned home from America in 1966 to get married. His plane hit an airpocket and dropped several hundred feet, scattering everything about the cabin. As I said earlier, he negotiated a deal with Jock Stein in 1968 that if we won by four goals against Red Star

Big shots in Houston, Texas! Kathryn and I with *(left to right)* Gillian, Gary and Jeff

A proud moment for me when I score for the Hurricanes in the Houston Astrodome

*Above* At Holyrood Palace after receiving the MBE, with Kathryn, Gillian, Gary and Jeff

*Opposite above* Champions again! We've just beaten Rangers 4-2 at Parkhead to clinch the 1979 Premier League title and give me a record eleventh championship medal

*Opposite below* My last game in the European Cup after eleven campaigns. We wave to the fans in the packed Santiago Bernabeu Stadium before playing Real Madrid in the quarter finals of the 1980 competition — we lost 3-2 on aggregate

Slightly pensive on my first day as coach at Celtic Park

Belgrade at Parkhead he would be excused flying to Yugoslavia, and he inspired us to a 5–1 win.

Then there was another trip to northern Finland and a place called Kokkola. It was just before this journey that his fear of flying rebounded on him. Because of the remoteness of the area we had to charter a small plane. Jets were out! When we arrived at Glasgow airport Jimmy was in a good enough humour and remained so until the flight was called.

When we got downstairs to the large sliding doors the little turbo-prop was warming up and Jimmy began to give the impression he didn't fancy flying to the Arctic Circle in it. Suddenly he said, 'You're not going to believe this, but my throat's killing me.' I didn't. Then he turned to Big Jock and blurted out, 'I cannae go, I cannae go.' It was now the manager's turn for the hot flushes and he thundered in that voice of his, 'Get on that bloody plane.' That ended the conversation abruptly and we all got on. A jet would have taken about three hours but this midget of a plane was to take five, and by the time we got there there was no point in training – we were shattered.

None more than Jimmy, who by this stage had been examined by Dr Fitzsimmons. Doc diagnosed heavy flu and came back to inform the manager, 'That's him ordered to bed till we leave for home.' Jimmy never left the hotel and was then flown home lying across a few seats. Had anyone else complained at Glasgow there would have been an immediate examination but, because of his fear of flying, no one had believed him.

Later in the seventies he got more confidence in the air but before that it was murder. He'd be at the chapel on the morning of a flight and he carried a small bottle of holy water with which he practically blessed each plane. I often wondered what would happen if he lost or forgot that particular bottle!

Another story shows just how bad his nerves were at that time. We were sitting at 30,000 feet, returning from a trip, when we encountered some bad turbulence. At such a moment everyone wants to talk just for the sake of saying something which will take their minds off the problem. The Wee Man was in such a state he turned to me and said, 'I wish they would put that red light on so I can fasten my safety belt.' The last word hadn't left his lips when he realized what he had said and the two of us roared with laughter all the way back to Glasgow.

He reckons his spell playing in American football helped cure him because there was a lot of flying involved there. Some airlines relaxed him with a rather inventive idea: they had a screen which the pilot would switch on to show his own view coming into land. It sounds like a pretty good idea for people with flying nerves.

Another thing which helped settle him came towards the end of his career at Parkhead. He was invited into the cockpit and I tagged along. The pilot showed him into the copilot's seat and asked him if he would like to fly the aircraft. It was a BAC 1–11 and you should have seen the Wee Man's face. Off went the automatic pilot switch and he was told, 'You're in charge'. The pilot, obviously keeping a hand close to his own set of controls, instructed Jimmy on what action to take. He made the plane climb slightly and it was obvious he was thrilled to bits. So there's a bit of a revelation – Jimmy Johnstone in charge of a jetliner at 30,000 feet and doing a cool 500 miles an hour.

Despite being the best of pals I know that Jimmy holds one grudge against me – the fact that I stopped him scoring a hat trick in professional football, something he never managed to achieve. Jimmy knocked in a lot of singles and doubles and it seemed his dream was about to come true in a match against St Johnstone at Parkhead in October 1966. We were winning 3–1 with thirty minutes to go when he went on a run which took him past three men. The ball broke forward and thinking he had overrun it I lashed a shot into the back of the net for my own second goal. He was livid. At time up he was screaming in my ear, 'I'd have got to it, I'd have got to it.' Right enough when I saw the Monday papers there was a photograph showing the goalkeeper stranded and Jimmy just a couple of feet behind me. My life was a misery for weeks afterwards and the other lads would keep it going by winding him up. All would be quiet in the dressing room when somebody would say, 'You know, Jimmy, I reckon you would have reached that ball,' and it would start again. To this day he blames me, but if that's the worst fall-out we ever have then I'll be happy.

Jimmy Johnstone never scored a hat trick – but he flew an aeroplane! Pound for pound he was probably as brave a footballer as you would find anywhere. Against Atletico Madrid in 1974 he was constantly chopped to the ground but he'd get up, dust himself down and in the tradition of the best entertainers, just keep on going. You couldn't sicken or intimidate him. Occasionally I heard him say something like, 'That was a bad player I was up against.' But no defender could put him out of the game. He had tremendous balance and buoyancy and this helped him escape bad injuries. Even hefty tackles usually failed to stop him as he could stumble through them and be away before the defender recovered. His individual touches will always be remembered by the fans who saw him and I'll give an example of one which people often recall. It came in a game against Hibs at Easter Road. He was surrounded by players as Ronnie Simpson sent forward a long, high ball. The Wee Man watched it all the way, let it drop over his shoulder, caught it on his foot and never broke his stride. It was a fleeting but magical moment.

His orderings off were never provoked by him. He didn't go onto the park to kick people. Yet he was the supreme entertainer who sometimes didn't get the chance to show his skills. All he wanted was the ball at his feet to show the world what he could do. He was also a great critic of his own play and he would take it personally if the team was playing badly.

He had a great relationship on the field with Bobby Murdoch who really helped him turn on some of the great displays. Some supporters didn't appreciate Bobby's worth until he had departed Parkhead but he was always fully appreciated by the players.

John Clark was another who was highly thought of by his fellow professionals. He played away quietly and efficiently at the back while we were grabbing the headlines up front.

I suppose it's natural that fans will always take to the characters of the game ... people like Bertie Auld who would really turn on a show for them and sometimes overshadow the others.

The Wee Man was one of the game's great characters. If I had a pound for every mile I travelled with him I would be a rich man today.

But I'd rather have the memories.

# 9

# This is America

I was lapping the track at Celtic Park in training on a brisk January day in 1978 when I saw the burly figure of Jock Stein appear at the tunnel mouth. As I got closer he came out and shouted, 'Come here a minute, Lemon, I want a word with you.' I had an idea what was on his mind as it had been rumoured a couple of Scottish clubs were showing interest in me. But he took my breath away when he inquired, 'How do you fancy going to play in American football?' I told him I didn't like the idea one little bit. I wasn't interested. Remember, in my earlier days, Ardrossan had seemed a million miles from Saltcoats – America was out of the question.

But Jock always was a persistent man and a few days later he told me a couple of American clubs were showing interest in signing me. I realized by this time that my seventeen happy years at Parkhead were swiftly drawing to a close, especially when the manager said, 'You don't want to play for any club here other than Celtic, so you would be happier in the States and it will give you a wee break as well.' I told him I would talk it over with my wife Kathryn, who reckoned we should take the chance.

Knowing that my wife and kids would like the experience suddenly made the decision a lot easier and as the days went by I began warming to the idea myself. I went back in to see Jock at his office and gave him my decision. Sitting there with him was an unreal experience. We chatted away about America but neither of us mentioned the words 'freed' or 'released'. I think it was

117

a toss-up to see who was going to break down first – the Big Man or me. I had a lump in my throat and I'm sure he did too. We had been through so many good times together. We shook hands and I walked out the door feeling numb at the thought that my association with Celtic was over.

The team showing most interest in me was a new club just being set up in Texas called Houston Hurricane and Jock had told me that their coach Timo Liekoski was stopping off at Glasgow to see me as part of a recruitment mission to Europe. Kathryn and I went to meet him at Glasgow airport's Excelsior Hotel and immediately he impressed us as being 100 per cent genuine in his aims. He made me a very good offer in terms of both cash and conditions – more money in fact than I had ever earned with Celtic. But let me expose here the myth that everyone in American soccer makes a lot of money. I would say each club has around four players in the top salary bracket. Others get a reasonable deal but some of the American youngsters really struggle a bit to make ends meet. I was fortunate to be one of the elite at Hurricane, but America is not as lucrative as many think.

The initial moves for me had started in January 1978 but it was March before I was required to travel, which allowed me time to get my affairs in order. My last game for Celtic was a Reserve match against Motherwell at Celtic Park, in front of a handful of spectators, just the day before I flew out to Houston. We were down 3–0 at half-time but we fought back and I scored a penalty plus the equalizer with the game finishing at 3–3. That pleased me a lot. That night we packed our remaining suitcases and the following afternoon headed for Glasgow airport for our connecting flight to Gatwick.

As soon as I got to Glasgow I was paged. When I picked up the telephone it was Jock Stein. 'I'm at Prestwick airport to see you off,' he said. Poor Jock had thought I was on a direct flight and had gone to the wrong place. But to me it didn't matter. He had made a magnificent gesture which was typical of him. I had no hard feelings against

Jock because he had allowed me to leave Celtic, although, having said that, I certainly didn't feel I was finished. I was upset, and of course wanted to play on at Parkhead, but then so would anyone.

Anyway, I had a new part of my career to get on with. After our ten-hour flight to Houston, my feet hardly touched the ground and I realized the lifestyle could be pretty frantic. We landed on Thursday night and the following day I was training with my new team-mates, many of whom had also just arrived in the country. Next day – Saturday – we flew across to the West Coast where we were due to meet Los Angeles Aztecs on the Sunday. Having travelled something like 7000 miles in a couple of days I was glad to sit back and relax that Saturday night – and relaxation was very much the theme of Hurricane.

The club had booked us into the Pasedena Hilton's penthouse suites, where we tucked into the biggest steaks I'd ever seen and washed those down with a few bottles of lager – that was the done thing. We were still up and chatting at 11 p.m. whereas had I been at Seamill with Celtic curfew would have been a couple of hours earlier. That's the way they did things there and in our case it was good, because it gave us a chance to get to know one another.

Next day I found myself in opposition to George Best and Charlie Cooke in what proved to be a difficult debut for us. Our first shock came before kickoff time – the sponsors had failed to deliver our new jerseys!

We had to play in our training gear, which was quite suitable, but the red shirts we used had different numbers to those we had been allocated. The Americans are very strict about that so that spectators – many seeing soccer for the first time – can follow who's who. So Hurricane were fined over that little episode.

Shock number two was the late arrival of our goalkeeper who landed from Yugoslavia the morning of the match! He spoke no English at all. I remember just two minutes of the match had gone as I snatched a look at the stadium clock and Dario Maranovich came sailing off

119

his line for a cross ball and missed it. We were down 1–0 and I thought, Good start America. Meanwhile, we outfield players were trying hard to establish some kind of pattern and understanding and, at half-time, being still only one goal behind, we thought we had a chance. Timo, our coach, had a word with everyone except poor Dario We began the second half and again, with two minutes on the clock, over came a similar cross, out came Dario and missed it– and we were two down. I laid on a goal to bring it back to 2–1 but by this time the travelling was catching up fast with me and I felt really tired. However the lads stuck well to their task and we equalized with just ten minutes to go and held out– a really good performance. At the end I rushed over to Timo and told him I was so shattered I thought it better if I missed the thirty-five-yard shoot-out decider. What I didn't realize was that before that came about there had to be a period of extra time. I nearly fainted, but urged on by Timo and my own pride I staggered through those fifteen minutes. Meanwhile our keeper Dario had been living dangerously as he used some unorthodox methods to keep the ball out of the net and the match was still at 2–2.

As we prepared for the shoot-out the atmosphere was tense. Timo, with a jumble of words and gestures attempted to explain the mechanics to Dario. he nodded but I don't think any of us were convinced. Aztecs had the first kick and as their player began his run from the thirty-five-yard line Dario came rushing out like some great gorilla to block the attempt. We scored and kept scoring while Dario blocked again and again! We won and he was the hero of the crowd. After the game he had played it was unbelievable. But I'm afraid Dario had a short reign. After another eccentric performance he was sent packing.

I had played in that first match with an injured toe and found afterwards that I was practically crippled. They don't mess about in the States I was to discover. On arrival back at Houston I was whipped into hospital where our club doctor – Dr Matsu – strapped me to a couch before producing a scalpel. He made two incisions which released all the poison and almost caused my team-mate Ian Anderson – the former Dundee player – to pass out. What a start for me in American football. Dr Matsu then removed the entire toenail and gave me some painkillers the size of gob-stoppers saying rather ominously that I would need them. I took one there and then, but during the journey home the effects wore off and the pain was so bad I had to stick my foot out of the car window for some relief!

The second game was the local derby against Dallas Tornadoes – from a mere 400 miles away – in the magnificent Houston Astrodome. It was in this match that Dario sold the jerseys and we were 3–0 down after eighteen minutes.

The Astrodome was a marvellous place to play and to train. By pressing a few buttons in the master control room banks of seating would move, changing the shape from a baseball pitch to a soccer pitch. The giant electric scoreboard was also a sight to behold. Every time a goal was scored – or a home run at baseball – it burst into music and a type of firework display. At some grounds the scoreboard would adapt into a larger than life television screen giving a close-up of each player as he ran onto the field to take a bow before a match. It was a strange sensation to look up and see a massive portrait of yourself. At first I was very self-conscious of walking out on my own to the pitch but now I think the idea of introducing the players individually is good for the fans. The entire build-up to the game in the States is geared for the fans because they are, after all, the important people. Before each match the American national anthem is played and I always put my hand over my heart and sang the words which appeared on the scoreboard. I remember one American player asking me why I sang his anthem with such devotion. 'Because,' I told him, 'I'm taking your money.' He was impressed. Thank God I was never offered any roubles!

Anyway, back to the Astrodome and its advantages.

We could train there every day unaffected by the weather, unlike here where our unpredictable climate can do so much damage to training routines. The great thing about astroturf is that no matter how hard it is punished the ball always runs true. It's like playing on a carpet, but in matches you had to remember that the ball just wouldn't pull up, unlike on grass. It was a matter of timing a run past an opponent very carefully, otherwise you just ran the ball out of play. Another good spinoff is that players wear training shoes rather than leather boots so the injury problems have never been as serious as they are here. The drawback is certainly the burns you can suffer on the man-made surface.

But the advantages far outweigh the disadvantages and I think an astroturf surface helps players to develop their skills more. Celtic are fortunate now that Helenvale Park – near Parkhead – has a full-size astroturf pitch and I think it has helped the present players enormously with their skills.

Travel is a major part of the game there but the long flights never bothered me, especially with the attitude Americans have to air travel. We tend to turn up at airports hours before flights depart whereas Americans just turn up at the last minute and walk on. One of my team-mates left things a bit tight once though, and literally had to knock on the door to get on the plane just before the pilot pulled away from the terminal building! Another great advantage is that there are so many flights that if you miss one there's a good chance there'll be another one within the hour.

In my time with Hurricane I played in San Diego (Stompers), California (Surfs), Oakland (Stompers), Chicago (Stings), Detroit (Express), Boston (Teamen), Tampa Bay (Rowdies), Dallas (Tornadoes), Minnesota (Kicks), Tulsa (Roughnecks), Philadelphia (Furies), Denver (Cocaraba Caribou), Los Angeles (Aztecs) and Memphis (Rogues).

It was in Memphis that I scored my first goal in the States. Earlier that day I had made my way to the home of the late Elvis Presley as I was a great fan of his. Gracelands was closed that day because his body was being removed from the local cemetery and reburied in the grounds of his mansion. I only got as far as the gates but achieved an old ambition. I bought a postcard before leaving next morning and sending it to Jock Stein with the message, 'That's me done it all in football – visited Gracelands and scored a goal in Elvis's home town.'

Another amazing feature of my stay in America was a personal fan club of exiled Celts. Everywhere I went there would be a knot of them behind the goals wearing the green and white and singing, 'You'll Never Walk Alone'. I never did. At every one of the grounds I played at the exiles were there. At the end of the game they would be waiting outside to wish me all the best, and many of them told me I would return to Celtic. The American lads in the team got a real insight into what kind of tradition a team like Celtic had when they saw such shows of loyalty. They were impressed by the charisma, and said they hoped one day that soccer in America would inspire the same type of feeling. It was funny to see the American players shake their heads in disbelief when they saw the Celtic fans wherever we played, one would always come in and say, 'They're at the door to see you again.' Those fans were great – and so were the fans at our Kearney New Jersey club who made me a special presentation.

Our home life on the outskirts of Houston was very happy. The club gave us a fine flat with a swimming pool and other facilities for the kids. They also threw in a Japanese car complete with my name and the number 11 painted on the doors. There was a formal handing-over ceremony to the players, and as they all got into the cars I found I had walked round to the passenger side – forgetting the left-hand drive!

Kathryn and the kids settled down very quickly – especially when they discovered the wife of our next door neighbour was a girl from Ecclefechan in Dumfriesshire! The setting was perfect for bringing up a young family. My youngest son Jeff couldn't swim, yet within weeks was diving into the pool with confidence. Kathryn found out very quickly that Houston was made for women. The school bus would pick up the children at 8.30 in the morning and deliver them back at 3 p.m. All the women would be out shopping in the marvellous malls or at the local sports complex enjoying swimming, tennis and golf. The climate guaranteed a good outdoor life.

As a family we had a lot of fun. I remember after we had been there only a few days we decided to eat at McDonald's. About fifty yards from the actual eating place you had to stop the car, roll down the window and speak your order into a large grill on the wall. I felt a bit of a fool asking this thing for hamburgers, Cokes etc, in what had to be a posh voice so that they could understand me. I duly got through that ordeal and drove up to the collection point. I heard the voice say, 'Can I have your order, sir?' I explained I had already made it only to be told by the girl that she was talking through her microphone to someone further back in the queue! The kids exploded with laughter. We seemed to be together enjoying ourselves a lot of the time.

After matches the club would always hold a disco, which was also open to the fans. Kathryn and I would take the kids along and as often as not we would meet players and their wives from back home – people like George Best, Charlie Cooke and George Graham. I found the American fans were great. They never criticized you and I remember after a 3–0 defeat they complimented us on our play. Had I been with Celtic in such circumstances I'd have been frighted to show my face after a defeat like that. The fans were well looked after though by the club. Apart from the disco invites they were always handing out tee-shirts and pennants and making a fuss of the younger fans in an effort to encourage their attendance. We also held soccer clinics to help the kids understand the game.

The restaurants in the Astrodome were something else, you could have anything from a hamburger to a five-star meal. One morning at about 2 a.m. on the way back from an after-match disco we felt hungry and stopped for a meal. Kathryn kept saying no one at home would believe that we could get something to eat at that time. After that we often used to stop at a supermarket around 3 a.m. and get the next day's groceries. It was a very different lifestyle.

Obviously there are some aspects of American life which are not ideal in a family sense. We got to know a lot of local couples who were unhappy about their children growing up there because of the drugs scene. From experience I can tell you that drugs were easily come by. After matches, for instance, some of my American team-mates on occasion offered me one of their joints, but I always told them I preferred to relax with a couple of lagers. I'm not suggesting that drug-taking was rife amongst footballers but some obviously preferred to smoke pot than to have a couple of beers after a game. There's no doubt it is a problem for the kids because they have to go to school and mix with others, you just have to hope that through the example you give them they don't get themselves involved. Luckily we were never faced with that problem, as the kids were very young and only at school there for a short time. I suppose sunny Saltcoats is a healthier atmosphere in that respect.

On the playing side I had a 100 per cent record, taking part in all thirty matches – the only player to do this – and it gave me a chance to assess the good and the bad in the way the game is played there.

I was always one of the doubting Thomases about the game's chances of survival in the States, and the fact that Hurricane have gone out of business tends to support my point. If the Americans are to survive they must step into line with FIFA rules and play the game as the rest of us do. They have made two vital alterations: changing the markings on the field and making sure there can never be a drawn match. Getting a positive result may be good for the fans but I can tell you it's absolutely shattering for players to put in the kind of effort which merits a share of the points, only to have to take part in extra-time – called overtime there – then a shoot-out decider.

There are a lot of good players in American football but I feel the thirty-five-yard lines from goal – which mark the only offside areas – are killers. It destroys midfield play and a couple of experienced campaigners can tie things up quite comfortably. In my time there both Bobby Moore and Mike England were prime examples of players standing on these lines and intercepting well. It had to be a peach of a pass to drop behind them.

The make-up of the Hurricane team will, I'm sure, interest a lot of people. Rules state that there must be at least two Americans in the team. We had more than most, yet were still a fairly mixed bunch with an Argentinian, Yugoslav, Bermudan, Turk, West German and a couple of Scots. Despite the many tongues we got on well together. I think each of us knew we had an obligation to make the new club work. It hád no tradition and we felt we must get a level of morale which would give us the chance to compeɩe properly against the established outfits.

We tended to get together a bit more off the pitch than players do here at home and, apart from the after-match disco, we would gather on a Monday night at the Houston Memorial Park. We'd take our families, watch the young Houston players and then sit and chat.

Hurricane were always going to struggle for survival in the area though. There were probably 20,000 youngsters in Houston playing football. But on other nights of the week they would be playing the American games. You never saw kids playing with a few jackets for goalposts. Everything was organized for them. Monday was basket-ball, Tuesday tennis, Wednesday bowling and so on. Mainly they played games with their hands, and kicking a ball against a wall wasn't in their make-up.

Despite seeing the warning signs I enjoyed my season in Houston. As I said earlier we often had a couple of beers the night before a match – purely a social thing. (At Seamill it would have been a stroll followed by a cup of tea. The Americans had a different attitude – but they were responsible with it.) Anyway, when we visited a town or city for the first time we would try to find a quiet

spot to relax. In Chicago it was Flanagan's Bar! Next
morning Timo called us together for our pre-match talk
which we knew was going to be tough. It was our
twenty-ninth game of the season and we had to win the
last two to qualify for the play offs. Before starting, Timo
told us he had been in an Irish bar called Mooney's the
previous night and that he had been surprised not to have
seen some of us there. Then he began his talk, he was a
good tactician and a good speaker.

Born in Finland, he had married in the States and had
played a big part in coaching there from schools football
up to national team level. He was just unfortunate that he
didn't have enough good and established players on hand
at Houston. He was always very thorough in his approach
to games and had eight and nine-page reports prepared on
the opposition by assistants who would go and spy for
him. They contained everything from defensive ploys to
attacking ploys. Every player was detailed and his
strengths and weaknesses given. These reports would be
handed to us a few days before a match so we could study
them.

But that day he had only been speaking a couple of
minutes when he crashed a copy of the report against the
table and said, 'This costs us five hundred dollars a game
to produce. This is our twenty-ninth game and this is what
I think of this,' and he threw it in the bin. Then he said
with a frown, 'But if there's anything you want to know
about Chicago just ask me now.' The place was hushed as
I put up my hand and he said, 'Yes Bobby?'

I said, 'How do you get to Mooney's Bar?' All the
British lads were rolling about with laughter. The
American boys didn't quite get it. But Timo just cracked
up with laughter as well.

The tension was broken for everyone and he told us,
'Just go out and play to position and do your own thing.'
But the American players were unhappy at this. They like
to play to exact instruction. We played really well that
night and were unfortunate to lose 2–1 in overtime. We
lost so many games because of that extra period.

That result meant we needed nine points from our last game to reach the play offs for the Soccer Bowl. We had really made life difficult for ourselves as nine points is the maximum you can get from any game – and only after a lot of blood, sweat and tears. You had to win and score three goals to reach that target and it was during the last game that one of the flaws in the system was highlighted.

We met Tampa Bay Rowdies in the Astrodome and managed to get into a two-goal lead. At this point one more goal and we were home and dry. We were playing out of our skins and at half-time were in raptures in the dressing room. In the second half Tampa pulled back to 2–2. But goals against didn't matter. As long as we got that third goal we would qualify. But here's the weakness. If a team was only 1–0 ahead with say a few minutes to go they might consider selling a goal to take the match to overtime when they could have more time to search for the further goals needed and that can affect the outcome of results from elsewhere. I thought in that respect the game was a bit 'Mickey Mouse'.

In the event we lost that final game 2–3 and to be honest I was totally confused at the end of it over the points system. On the other hand it wasn't bad to know that if you lost 4–3 away from home having had a go you at least got three points. That encouraged positive play. Yet it could be a cruel game also. You could draw 0–0 and go into overtime and if it was still 0–0 and you lost say 3–2 in the shoot-out the opposition would get seven points and you got nothing. I remember one game in Detroit when a goal was scored in only forty seconds of overtime and that was it. Imagine how confusing this was out on the pitch! Here is how the system works:

You get six points for a win – no matter what the score is. On top of that you get a point per goal up to three – that gives a maximum nine points. So the ideal thing to do is to win a game 3–0. You get the same for that as for a 10–0 victory.

For a shoot-out victory you get the normal six points for a win but only one further point is added no matter how many of the shoot-out chances you convert.

As I've said there are good and bad points about the system but I think there is some merit in awarding points for goals within reason. Up to three I thought was a good idea.

Before leaving America let me give a word of warning to any British players who have thought about giving the game over there a try. There is, as I've explained, intense competition from the more traditional American sports. So the clubs want value for money from players they import from foreign countries. I know that some clubs have been soured by the experiences they've had with certain British players who've treated the whole thing as a holiday. If you don't pull out the stops they'll have you out on your ear.

But if you give 100 per cent there can also be problems. I had difficulty in regaining my registration papers when I returned to Scotland and there have been players who've got involved in wrangles between clubs through no fault of their own. Another drawback in the American contract system is that you can wake up in the morning and find you have been traded to another club – or even find your entire club has been sold and transferred to another city.

Our Turkish winger was there one day and the next he had been traded to San Diego even though he was not in favour of the deal. It's the general managers who run the clubs – not the coaches who are the equivalent of our team managers – and they often make players toe the line.

I remember after one game in Denver our flight was delayed, and after being on the road for ten hours and arriving back in Houston at 2 a.m. we were ordered to attend a photocall at 9 a.m. Business was business. Sleep came second.

One final drawback I felt was the NASL rule against paying bonus money. I think that type of incentive is required if the States are ever to compete seriously with the rest of the world. The result there at present is that too many players pick up their wages without giving any great effort and that's bad for the future of the game there.

My American experience lasted from March 1978 until August of that year. I was very touched by the fact that practically all of my team-mates came round to my flat the day we were leaving.

I had enjoyed every minute of my stay with the Hurricane but when I headed back to Scotland I had to come to terms with the fact that I was no longer a Celtic player.

# 10

# Indian Summer of Glory

The constant drone of the engines at 38,000 feet above the Atlantic made sleep impossible and it seemed the nine-hour non-stop flight from Houston, Texas to London was unending. But rest was out of the question in any case. My mind was in turmoil, my future uncertain. Returning to Scotland and my native Saltcoats appealed greatly to me after five months playing in the North American Soccer League, but for the first time in more than fifteen years I suffered the torture of knowing that there would be no return to my other home – Celtic Park.

Timo Liekoski, head coach of Houston Hurricane, had made me a great offer to stay on in America for the following season but I had turned it down. He even offered to pay my salary if I would do some scouting in Scotland for him then return the following summer. But I told him that, at the age of thirty-five, it was important for me to keep playing competitive matches. I knew through the grapevine that several clubs in Scotland were showing interest in my future and my co-author Gerry McNee, who spent some time with me in Texas, had suggested that with Billy McNeill taking over from Jock Stein as manager it was possible that Celtic might ask me back. But I never really thought it would happen.

When I arrived back home a few offers did indeed come my way. Kilmarnock and Ayr both contacted me and they were, after all, handy for me living in Ayrshire. But I also got a call from Parkhead telling me to hold fire and wait for further contact.

Just a few days later I went to Cappielow to watch Celtic play Morton in the opening game of the season and the first man I met was the man who had freed me six months earlier – Jock Stein – and his first question was, 'Are you going back to Parkhead?' Obviously things were moving behind the scenes. It was just a few days before Jock's testimonial match against Liverpool and about a week or so before he was to sever his connections with Celtic and move to Leeds United. He had wanted me to play in his benefit but I had asked to be excused because of jet-lag.

Then Billy McNeill phoned me and I went back to Celtic Park for a meeting with him. I vividly remember his opening words, 'Look, this might only be a short-term thing. I need help till I can get hold of some new players. It could be a month, two months or longer.' Kilmarnock and Ayr would have given me a signing-on fee but at Parkhead the deal was a straightforward wage. Hand on heart, though, all I wanted to do was play again for Celtic. Yet after signing up again I began to wonder if the day would ever dawn when I could pull on the jersey and run back out in front of those fans.

Several newspaper stories both here and in the United States caused confusion and I couldn't get clearance from Hurricane to resume my career at Parkhead. Eight agonizing weeks passed. We would phone or telex Houston asking for my clearance papers. Houston would tell us they were at NASL headquarters in New York who in turn would tell us they were back in Houston. I heard that the general manager of Houston was determined to have me back there, which was a great compliment but a real pain as well. Finally I wrote him a letter stating that if I ever returned to the States Hurricane would have first call on my services. As it turned out, they were to go bust a short time later and end media speculation that I had signed a three-year contract. My only promise to Houston earlier that year had been to play for a full season and that had been honoured.

Still, time went by and it was murder training every day

without kicking a ball for real and I knew with each passing week that the team would get stronger and make it all the more difficult for me to win back a place.

At last Houston agreed to my plea and at last I made my comeback in a reserve game at Easter Road. The lesson was that it's nice to go abroad and play, but it can land you in all sorts of bother. If a foreign club wants to be difficult it can take an age to get things sorted out.

So what did it mean to be back with Celtic? I just couldn't believe it. You could say it was like walking out of a nightmare into a world of nice dreams. Six months or so earlier I had walked out of Parkhead with an empty feeling, quite unable to grasp the fact that it was all over. Now I was part of the club again. Little did I know at that point that I was to enjoy a real Indian summer of glory and win two medals which would make me a record-breaker in both the Scottish League championship and the Scottish Cup.

I didn't play too many matches in that first season back and towards the end Billy McNeill and I had another meeting where he hinted at a possible parting of the ways. But then a crucial pattern developed which was to lead to yet another season. Celtic had struggled in the championship race and we had been knocked out of the Scottish Cup at Parkhead by Aberdeen. It looked that night as though we were heading for a blank season. The Dons had taken a 2–0 lead and although I had come on as sub and scored a goal we lost 2–1. But that appearance seemed to do the trick and I began a run of matches where I went on as substitute and cracked in a few rather vital goals. The championship, though, still seemed a remote possibility.

It really boiled down to the fact that we had to win every match on the run-in. Two real nail-biting occasions I remember at that time came at Firhill on a holiday Monday and then at Ibrox against St Mirren on a Friday night.

We had just scraped home against Partick Thistle after being a goal behind. St Mirren had hired Ibrox for their match with us because Love Street was under reconstruction, and playing on a Friday night was a bit of an unreal experience. We led 1–0 into the second half but the form was not convincing and the nerves apparent. I was sent on as a sub and scored a second goal which was met more with relief than joy. Back in the dressing room afterwards Billy McNeill came over to me, sat down and spoke words which were sweet as music to me, 'I've been thinking about you again. You could still be at Celtic Park again next year. You probably wouldn't be a regular but you could be a great help to the lads coming off the bench as you've been doing recently.'

My reply was simple and immediate: 'I'd be delighted.'

That result against St Mirren plus rearrangement of fixtures and an extension to the league season had set us up for what was to be one of the greatest games of my long career – a championship decider against Rangers at Celtic Park. Monday, 21 May 1979 is an evening I'll never forget. From being virtual also-rans we were suddenly in a position where victory would give us the title. I was again on the bench and early in the match suffered agonies as we went down 1–0. Worse was to follow when Johnny Doyle got his marching orders after an incident with Rangers scorer McDonald. It was a moment which was to change the whole complexion of the match and a moment which brought me into the thick of battle. It had been terrible sitting in the dugout and, in fact, I think I spent a fair bit of the time warming up on the track. It was always a good idea to be ready and not struggling to get your second wind when the time came to play.

Immediately the ordering off came, Billy McNeill and John Clark took a bold gamble. They took off a defensive player – Mike Conroy – and sent on an attacker – me. Billy shouted my instructions as I wriggled out of my tracksuit, 'Tell Davie (Provan) to fall back and play behind you. I want you and George (McCluskey) to push onto their back men and work them as hard as you can.'

Well, it worked because Roy Aitken, my big pal from Ayrshire, did his Roy of the Rovers act and equalised, then McCluskey put us 2–1 ahead. What a match he had that night. His stamina was incredible. But within a minute of McCluskey making it 2–1, Rangers were level at 2–2. They got a corner and as the ball came over, Tom McAdam went up, but his header glanced away in the direction of Bobby Russell. I was in the middle of a ruck of players as his shot whizzed past me then I heard the dreaded dull thud and looked round to see the ball coming off the post and flashing into the opposite corner. There were only ten minutes to go and a point was no use to us. I remember thinking, We're battling to get this one now. But in the back of my mind I knew we could do it. The first thing that had struck me when I entered the game was that Rangers were struggling physically. I found I was getting past men with ease.

With time running out we got the break which was to win us the championship. George McCluskey cut in from the right and hit the ball across goal. Rangers' centre-half, Colin Jackson, stuck out a foot, knocked the ball past Peter McCloy and agonizingly it crossed the line. It's not often you feel sorry for an opponent in the heat of battle but I did have a twinge of sympathy for Jackson. He had to carry the burden of losing that vital goal, yet had he left the ball either Johannes Edvaldsson or I would have scored. We were queueing up for a shot when George crossed.

There were just minutes to go and the tension was showing everywhere. I ran the length of the field and headed the ball away for a corner as Rangers threw everyone forward in a last effort. Then to my horror I saw the cross come over, again glance off Tom McAdam's head and again land at the feet of Bobby Russell. I thought, Not again. My heart missed a beat but it didn't stop me getting my boot, with some others, into blocking the shot. Suddenly we were breaking forward and had an advantage of four against two.

Murdo McLeod had the ball and I was running wide on his right shouting for the pass. I wanted to take the ball to the corner flag and play for possession. Then I saw Murdo wind back his leg and I shouted, 'Send it to the back of the terracing.' Not Murdo. He sent a screaming and unsavable shot right over the head of McCloy into the roof of the net.

It was a goal which will live with me for ever, not only because of the awesome power of the shot but also because of the reaction on the field. No one ran to the scorer. Instead everyone sagged to the ground in utter relief.

Then there was a feeling of tremendous elation as the final whistle sounded, within seconds of that goal, and we all ran to Murdo. It was a sensational moment and the 50,000 crowd, practically all Celtic supporters, went absolutely wild with delight. It was the greatest night at Parkhead since we had returned in triumph with the European Cup in 1967. I had gone through the nine consecutive championships in the Jock Stein era plus the first Premier League we had won in 1977. But none of them had been clinched at Celtic Park. So this was special. A night to savour for both players and fans.

We eventually got to the dressing rooms where the scenes were fantastic. I was sitting stripped to the waist, drinking a bottle of lager, when someone told me that Jimmy Johnstone was at the door looking for me. I went out and there was the Wee Man wearing a smile as big as his heart and full of congratulations for an old pal. That was one of the great features of the night. So many former players had turned up and were relishing the victory as though they too had been on the park.

I had to leave Jimmy after a few minutes because we were told the crowd wanted us back out for a lap of honour. So it was back on with the sweat-soaked jerseys and down the tunnel to a fabulous roar. When we had satisfied the crowd's demands we went back inside for a night of celebration. Celtic are a wonderful club for keeping links with their former servants. The tradition of the club has been built by its great players and it was good to see them welcomed back that night.

That match had been the final act of the season for us, and I was a contented man in the knowledge that I would still be a part of Celtic in the months ahead. Call it fighting for your very existence if you like, but what I had achieved towards the end of that season had impressed the people behind the scenes at Parkhead and had won me more time with the only club that mattered to me. On the morning after the championship Billy McNeill told my co-author Gerry McNee, 'There will always be a place here for people like Bobby Lennox.' Gerry told me afterwards that there had been a strong hint there that even when I decided to retire there would be a role for me at Parkhead.

While that particular conversation had been taking place in the manager's office I had been happily posing for photographs out on the park, holding up the number 11 sign used in substitutions to signify my eleventh championship medal – a record for Scottish football and a very proud moment for me.

The club responded generously to our win by arranging a week's holiday for the boys in Spain, a very good idea because, apart from the fun we had there, it also let the younger lads get to know each other that bit better, as there had been no European travel the previous season.

But there was to be a bit of travel at the start of the new season -- 1979–80 – when the first round of the European Champions' Cup draw paired us with a name which held no fond memories at Celtic Park – Partizani Tirana of Albania. It was because that club withdrew from the competition in 1967–8 that Celtic, as champions, had to forfeit their first round bye and instead had to take on the might of Russian champions Dynamo Kiev, who had given us an early knock-out.

The Albanians have always been a bit of a law unto themselves and more than once have withdrawn a club from European competition at the last minute and without explanation. We were to find out once again just how unpredictable they could be. They restricted the numbers of our party and banned the Scottish press from travelling with us.

Our chairman Desmond White was unhappy about the press situation. But when he attempted to get backing from UEFA he got a shock. Instead of threatening the

Albanians with expulsion it was Celtic who got the threat from Berne and at the end of the day we had to accept the situation, no matter how grudgingly. Newspaper men flew back and forward to Paris for weeks trying to extract visas from the Albanian Embassy there but without luck. The *Scottish Daily Express*, however, pulled off a bit of a coup by 'signing up' our director Kevin Kelly who turned sports writer for the afternoon; he even managed to get an open line from the stadium to the *Express* during the entire ninety minutes! There's absolutely no truth in the rumour that his report was slightly biased in favour of Celtic!

Tirana was a rather strange place to stay in; there didn't, for instance, seem to be any shops or cars. But I must say the people were extremely courteous and friendly, although we had been a bit on edge during the journey because there had been reports in the press about the Albanians' strict laws against long hair and beards (our captain Danny McGrain was a bit worried about the latter).

In the evening we would often go out for a walk along a main street which was miles long and incredibly wide. At that time of day it was packed, people just seemed to walk up one side and down the other in almost military fashion. (The telly was obviously hopeless as a form of entertainment – if indeed they had television! – and a drive in the country an impossibility.) Everyone linked arms with their partner whether it was man and woman or man and man or woman and woman! We were dressed smartly but casually in the likes of denims and were very conspicuous compared to their rather drab clothing. But as I said there was no hostility, in fact the opposite.

This was proved on the following day when we went to the stadium for our first training session – a quite extraordinary experience. The main stand was packed with around 10,000 people who roared and urged us on during our practice game and applauded the goals. When we got outside, our bus was surrounded by the entire crowd. I'd never seen anything like it for a mere training session. And there, beside the bus, was one man attempting to control the crowd. He was dressed in a blue uniform and looked very officious indeed. He started throwing punches and actually drove the crowd back across the huge square outside the stadium. But once we were all safely aboard they surged around again much to his annoyance. I started waving my fist and making a face at him. The crowd roared with delight because by the time he turned round to see what was amusing them I was looking innocently the other way. I kept this going for quite a few minutes and I'm sure if the driver hadn't moved off I could have formed the first Bobby Lennox fan club in Albania.

The game itself was a disappointment in that we lost 1–0, but never at any stage did their standard of play worry me. I knew we would win through in the return leg. They actually scored first in Glasgow to take a 2–0 lead but we went on to a comfortable victory and moved onto the second round draw for what, on paper, looked a fairly straightforward tie. We drew the Irish champions Dundalk who certainly gave us a fright and cost us a few fingernails over the two matches.

The first leg against Dundalk came in Glasgow, where we managed to beat them by only 3–2. Our pride was really hurt as there were media reports that their manager allowed them out on the Guinness on the night before matches, and that as part-timers they had a happy-go-lucky approach to football. There was certainly never any over-confidence on our part but sometimes it can creep into a team subconsciously no matter how hard you try to keep it out of your mind.

I thought we could beat them in Dundalk but when we got there we realized we were in for a real fight. Tractors had been brought in the previous night to build up the terracing and it seemed everyone in Ireland was going to be there. Bricks and planks of wood were hastily erected and when we took the field the place was crammed with people. The atmosphere and the pitch itself provided great levellers and showed how a professional team can become as disorganized as we became that night. Luckily

Danny McGrain recovered from injury to play and his influence was crucial. The man has great composure and can attack as well as he can defend and there's no doubt the team misses him when he's not there – and earlier that day we had thought he wouldn't be able to play.

Early in that match I hit an effort off the bar; at that precise moment I knew we had a battle ahead. If only that had gone in I'm sure we would have run out comfortable winners. Instead we found ourselves going into the last few minutes of the match still only a goal in front, but knowing that if they scored, their away goals would take them through to the quarterfinals. Everything, it seemed, was going wrong. I remember, for instance, that when a free kick flew across our goal Davie Provan was the last man jumping and that should never have happened. We just didn't know where we were. Then their right-back came thundering through to meet the ball at point-blank range as our keeper Peter Latchford came out. And it was only the Irishman's tired legs that saved us. I shouted, 'Who's picking him up?' I thought I had exonerated myself from any blame because I was sure he was the number four. As we argued among ourselves he turned round and he was their number two – the man I was supposed to mark! I felt a right idiot and got a well-deserved rollicking after the game. As I said, it just showed how a team of professionals could get caught out and it was a valuable lesson for all of us – even me at that late stage of my career.

Having survived that experience we went into the draw for the quarterfinals and drew the European Cup's greatest-ever ambassadors – Real Madrid. Everyone at Celtic Park got a fantastic lift at the thought of these ties. Here indeed was a great challenge for a young team. And the lads rose to it with a great 2–0 first leg win at Parkhead. You couldn't have asked for a better result.

Some people criticized us for our first-half performance that night. But I didn't think we were under pressure, although I agree we didn't get forward as much as perhaps we should have done. They made a lot of fancy passes across the field but I only remember one real effort from their coloured English striker, Laurie Cunningham. But George McCluskey and Johnny Doyle got two tremendous goals and set us up with a real chance of reaching the semifinals.

We travelled to Madrid with hopes high. I honestly didn't think we could get beaten – certainly not by three goals. But we hadn't reckoned on getting quite such a raw deal as we actually got. Within the first couple of minutes I almost had my knee-cap smashed by a shocker of a tackle. Then Johnny Doyle was almost halved in two by another challenge which brought no response from the referee.

Despite that we took the game to Real, we made chances and we even hit the bar. With just seconds to half-time we still held our two-goal advantage when the referee gave a bad decision against Peter Latchford for alleged time-wasting. Even after that he allowed further time, during which Real scrambled the ball over the line. The goal couldn't have come at a better time for them – or at a worse moment for us. But back in the dressing room experienced players like McGrain, Aitken and myself kept impressing on the younger lads that we were still a goal ahead with only forty-five minutes to go and that wasn't a bad position to be in.

But in the second half we just didn't play and finally lost 3–2 on aggregate. The experience for the younger players had been invaluable but it was a hard lesson to learn at the same time. We had allowed ourselves to be upset at a crucial stage. Tommy Burns had set up a chance for me but a Spanish defender took the ball away with his arm – and escaped what should have been a penalty. After that we had never got our heads up again.

The scenes in the dressing room were sad indeed. Several young players wept openly in the knowledge that a good chance had been lost and knowing that good chances in football can be rare.

As it turned out it was my last game in Europe. What a pity it had to be such an occasion – especially in a stadium where I had experienced victory much earlier in my career and had scored the winning goal. It took a while to get over that match and some people reckon it had an effect on our championship form at home where we surrendered a good lead to Aberdeen. Did Real undermine our confidence that much? It's hard to say. It didn't affect me but possibly it did the younger players and gave some doubts about their ability.

We dropped point after point in the league race, but in a bad streak like that you always think it will come to an end and we kept battling. The Dons had to come to Parkhead and win twice so we had to fancy our chances of winning at least one of those matches. But we didn't, and to make matters worse I missed a penalty in the first match after coming on as substitute.

Tom McAdam had been concussed just before half-time and on his way back onto the field had to turn back. The game was restarting and I had to rush to get on. When the penalty came I knew exactly where I wanted to put the ball, but made the mistake which has haunted golfers since the beginning of time. I lifted my head. The result was that I mishit the ball and the keeper saved. I think it's worth recording here that throughout my career I never once put a penalty wide. Either a keeper or a post stopped those which failed to hit the net.

In the end Aberdeen pipped us for the championship and all credit to them because they were a good side. It had been a strange campaign in that we had taken three points from them at Pittodrie and they had taken four from us at Celtic Park. The final, bizarre act of the championship for us came at Love Street, Paisley against St Mirren in our last game when we were awarded a penalty kick and then had the decision withdrawn. We lost a point while Aberdeen thrashed Hibs 5–0 at Easter Road and it was finally all over.

However the Scottish Cup was to save the season for us. In fact it had seen us produce the real Celtic spirit and tradition. We had been held by St Mirren in the quarter final at Parkhead. When I say held, it's worth pointing out that they led 1–0 until Murdo McLeod scored a dramatic equalizer just minutes from the end. So we faced the replay at Love Street on Wednesday night when obviously there was terrific interest in such a sudden-death situation.

We arrived at the ground around 6.30 p.m. and the place was teeming with people. The adrenalin soon began flowing and I had a feeling it was going to be quite a night. St Mirren started off really well and took the lead. To be honest we were struggling at that point. Our cause took a further setback when Tom McAdam was sent off. But once again a Celtic team down to ten men proved, as so often in the past, to be unbeatable. Doyle equalized but Saints went ahead from a penalty. Then we got a spot-kick which I took and I remember wasting no time about it as I rolled it into the net. It's best not to think about penalties – just run up and hit them.

That took this remarkable tie to extra time when Johnny Doyle scored a tremendous winner which convinced me that we were well on the way to winning the Cup. In the closing stages I remember being terrified in case I made a mistake, because we were on the verge of a truly great result, one we had worked really hard to produce. I was thirty-six years of age and Danny McGrain was no spring chicken either, but we had come through two hours of seething cup-tie pressure – and I had been freed two years earlier that very month!

We went on to meet Hibs in the semifinal, also a match with special memories – not only of my scoring the first goal in our 5–0 win. The great George Best had been signed by the Edinburgh club that season; during that game it was obvious he had retained his skills even if the legs had gone a bit and his midriff increased.

I would like to go on record as saying that I always found George Best a lovely fellow. Sure we've all read the articles of wild exploits and the rest but I have a cardinal rule in my life that I take people as I find them. I spent some time with him when I played in the North American

Soccer League, and after we had opposed one another on the field we would share a few beers. He was great company and my family were really thrilled one evening when he sat and chatted to them for ages. At the end of his stay with Hibs I remember reading a newspaper article by him in which he had named Danny McGrain, Bobby Clark and yours truly as the best professionals in the Scottish game. I was really flattered by that.

The day of the semifinal he tried hard to get the Hibs boys involved and sprayed some fabulous passes about. Being on the field beside him you got a real insight into his genius. At one stage he dummied me so well I had to pay to get back in! Despite his efforts the younger boys failed to read his moves and I remember his shaking his head and giving me a look of resignation. He wasn't being bigheaded or conceited. That's not his style. It was merely the fact that he knew, as I knew, that he should be playing in higher company. Hibs were struggling and fighting a losing battle against relegation. You were left to wonder what kind of asset he could have been to the likes of Celtic. You can never hide class and he had an abundance of it. I would have loved the opportunity to play alongside him even in that autumn of his career.

So we had reached the Scottish Cup final and, already holding the record, we had the chance to go for the club's twenty-sixth win in the competition. But once again Rangers blocked our path, and we knew it wouldn't be easy especially as our two central defenders, Roddy MacDonald and Tom McAdam, were unavailable because of suspension. Roy Aitken and Mike Conroy took their roles with Conroy being asked to do a special job out of position.

In the event he performed tremendously well against the aerial menace of Derek Johnstone. Roy Aitken too was immense that day. It was a hard game but a particularly good one in a footballing sense. I've often watched it since on video and it could easily have ended 6–6. It was real end-to-end stuff and in the closing minutes it could have gone either way. I came off the bench and we went into extra time still locked at 0–0. Then the breakthrough came when Danny McGrain tried a long-range shot which George McCluskey deflected. McCloy, the Rangers goalkeeper, got a hand to the ball but it bounced over the line and the Cup was ours. On that video tape there is a lovely moment at the end. Right on the final whistle the cameras closed in on our keeper Peter Latchford who wore a marvellous smile which just captured the moment of triumph. Peter, of course, has always enjoyed Old Firm matches more than most, coming from the south. He was always that bit more detached from the situation.

As I walked up the steps to the winners' rostrum I was the proudest man in Hampden because here I was receiving my eighth Scottish Cup medal (my sixth winner's medal) – another individual record to add to the eleventh championship medal of the previous season. What added to the pleasure of these late honours is that they had been gained against our greatest rivals – Rangers. This was indeed my Indian summer of glory. When you think how many players have battled for years and won nothing, here was I, having been written off two years earlier, still adding to my medal collection. It's at moments like that I appreciate just how good football, and life in general, has been to me.

We left Hampden and went back to a private reception at Celtic Park with our wives and families. It was a proud moment for me as my son, Gary, and John Clark's son, Martin, carried the Cup in through the front door and into the trophy room.

Amidst all the happiness that night it was as well I didn't know that I had in fact played my last competitive game for Celtic. It would have been a great occasion to announce my retirement – while still at the very top. Billy McNeill had done just that minutes after Celtic had beaten Airdrie in the 1975 Scottish Cup final.

But I felt good enough to keep going and after a quiet close season I returned for what should have been season number three of my Indian summer.

I got through the pre-season training without any problems and I remember a compliment from Billy McNeill when he said, 'I thought I'd see a flaw in your training this time, but there's none.' I was still fast and, without being bigheaded, I can tell you that a few of the younger players would join me if they wanted to step up their work. I still felt capable and confident of taking on opponents and showing them a clean pair of heels. I was always a great believer in the saying that you only get out of football what you put into it and that's why I played till the age of thirty-six. If you don't work hard and give 100 per cent commitment to your club, you're wasting your time.

In a pre-season match in Germany we were playing an amateur team and were well ahead when the manager decided I should go on for a spell. I had been bothered by a groin strain off and on since the end of the previous season. It had started in the remarkable match at Dens Park when we lost 5-1 to a Dundee team who got five chances and took them all, only to be relegated the following week. But I had played in the Cup final and was re-signed for season 1980-1 which would take me into my thirty-seventh year and my twentieth as a professional with Celtic. Billy McNeill asked me, 'How is that leg of yours?' I reckoned it was a bit better and played in the closing stages, scoring a goal from thirty yards – which was never quite my range! But I felt twinges and decided to rest again till we got back to Glasgow.

Little did I know that the spectacular thirty-yarder, for which I had taken some kidding from the other lads, would be my last for Celtic.

A few days after we got home Billy McNeill asked me to go to Barrowfield with our youth coach, Jim Lumsden, and give the youngsters a work-out. He took the defenders and I took the forwards and we began a few routines. One of the lads couldn't master the set-piece we were working on and I decided to demonstrate for him. As the ball came into the goalmouth I took four steps and felt this great ripping across my lower abdomen. I broke into a terrible

146

sweat and had just enough strength to get to my car and drive back to Parkhead.

Within four days I was black from the knee right up past the groin and across my stomach. Our physio, Brian Scott, worked hard and I kept up my hopes that it would clear. I had fought my way back into the top team against the odds in the previous few seasons and I still wanted to win medals. But after a visit to a specialist I got the news I always dreaded. He was quite adamant when he told me, 'This might never clear up. The bone is ragged and the ligaments may never heal.'

So what is it like to receive news like that after playing so many years at the top level? I didn't believe it, you don't believe things like that. Brian Scott continued to do his best for me but I was losing the battle.

Then late in the year came decision time for me. Frank Connors left the club to manage Berwick Rangers and Billy McNeill called me into his office to tell me the reserve team coach job was mine if I wanted it. He also warned me that he couldn't hold it indefinitely and it was a job which might not again be available to me.

I drove home to Saltcoats with a heavy heart and a lot on my mind. I sat with my wife, Kathryn, and talked it over. She cried for me that night because she knew just how much the game of football meant to me. But there could only be one decision and I took it. On the Friday morning I had been a footballer with Celtic Football Club. On the Saturday afternoon I was coach of Celtic reserves at Fir Park, Motherwell. And I was terrified.

Jim Lumsden actually took charge that day and had it not been for him I wouldn't have got through that day or the difficult days which followed. It was a big adjustment for me and I was thankful that Jim was always there to help and give me a bit of advice from his experience with the youth team. I'm lucky in that he and I share the same sense of humour and we have developed a good relationship with each other.

So another chapter of my career had ended and a new one was about to dawn but the most important thing of all was that I still belonged to the greatest club in the world.

# 11

# A Medal From the Palace

Just a few weeks before the news was broken to me about my playing career being over, I arrived home to the surprise of my life. I had left Parkhead after training and driven back to Saltcoats in the gathering gloom of a wintry November day. Just another normal day – or so I thought. When I opened the front door the first thing I saw was a rather large and imposing envelope on the hall table. When I turned it over and saw the crest I got the feeling it must be something very, very important.

My wife Kathryn appeared from the kitchen, having waited patiently for my arrival to find out its contents. I opened it carefully and removed what felt like a very expensive piece of paper.

I was stunned as I read the words, 'If offered the MBE would you accept it?' There was also a request that the offer be kept top secret until any announcement from Buckingham Palace. I was absolutely thrilled, and I accepted by return post! It had never crossed my mind that I should be given such an honour and, without sounding too sugary about it, I felt it was another great milestone for the Celtic Football Club. It's a great thing for the individual involved but it's also a recognition of a club's achievements.

Following my acceptance I heard not another word until the last day of 1980 when a newspaperman rang up to ask for a photograph of the Lennox family. Even then I didn't realize what was behind the request. During the past couple of years there had been similar requests as newspapers did stories about me – the veteran – going into yet another year. Then the reporter said, 'You have heard the news, haven't you?' My name had been published in the New Year's Honours List which goes out to the various newspapers a day in advance. So it had come to pass after all! But after that flurry of activity and many wishes of congratulations all went very quiet again.

Then a few months later I received another letter telling me that the investiture would take place at Holyrood Palace, Edinburgh on 7 July. On both counts I was very happy. The fact that it was in Edinburgh made it easier to take the entire family, and secondly it was the birthday of my late father, one of the greatest men I ever knew. I think Kathryn would have preferred Buckingham Palace – and what woman wouldn't, because there cannot be many experiences like entering that building for an investiture. But we all realized that Edinburgh meant we could take the kids and both mums.

On these occasions you are allowed two guests plus a third special guest. It was agreed by everyone that Kathryn and my two older children, Gillian and Gary, would accompany me into the palace itself while the two grandmothers looked after young Jeff on the fringe of the proceedings.

At last the great day dawned and we left Saltcoats early in the morning, intending to stop off at a hotel en route for a coffee and a chance to freshen up. But as luck would have it we hit a bad traffic jam as we joined the M8. There was a huge tailback with police in attendance, and time started to run away from us. I began to panic at the thought of giving the Queen – to use that quaint Glasgow phrase – 'a dizzy'. I managed to attract the attention of a police inspector and luckily he was a football man and seemed to recognize me. I explained my predicament and he told me to pull out and he would make sure a police motor cyclist got us clear.

We were off and running again but late and by the time we reached Edinburgh we realized just how much the clock was against us. About two hundred yards from the palace – going down the Royal Mile – Kathryn suddenly reminded me that she had still to change into her dress! Between that and what was to happen over the next hour or so you'll gather that the Lennox family aren't too experienced when it comes to meeting the Queen! I stopped the car to ask for final directions and at that point noticed a quiet looking close. Although it had been raining for a while, it was nice and dry and we decided that that would be the dressing room.

I stood there on guard – top hat to keep the rain off my head, plus tails. I felt a right idiot and the kids were roaring with laughter. Kathryn and her mum had vanished up the close and then emerged a few minutes later giggling like a couple of schoolgirls.

Just moments after that little drama we were sweeping through the palace gates with our large, official car-parking pass gaining us access to the inner sanctum. We left our mothers and Jeff in the quite splendid gardens in the care of the staff there and we went on inside.

Everything was meticulously and brilliantly arranged. Kathryn and the children were taken straight to the investiture room while I was directed elsewhere. They had separate rooms for knighthood recipients, CBEs, OBEs and, in my case, the MBE. I sat down carefully so as not to crease my tails when, to my embarrassment, I realized I was the only one still with a top hat! Everyone else had checked theirs in at the front door downstairs so, red faced, I had to ask permission to leave the room.

A few minutes later we all heard the national anthem strike up and everyone got to their feet. We couldn't see the Queen at this point as she had entered the main room. Then we were all shuttled forward in alphabetical order towards the investiture room.

As the 'Ls' were called forward I was amazed to see that the MBE immediately in front of me was a Thomas Lafferty from Saltcoats – a lad who had been a year in front of me at school in our home town. What a coincidence – and what a day for the town we both love so well. I hadn't seen him for years and we shook hands warmly. My MBE was for services to the Celtic Football Club while his was for work in the oil industry.

With almost military precision we were gradually moved forward from one steward to another, had our names checked, and then moved to the door of the investiture room and for the first time got a glimpse of the Queen.

She was on a slightly raised platform – just a couple of inches above the floor. We had all been given our instructions: walk up the left side of the room, turning at a right angle till in front of her, then face her and bow. Robert Lennox was called and moved off at a slower than usual pace along the left trying not to bump into the Royal Company of Archers who – without an arrow in sight – provided the guard of honour. I overshot the runway a bit and as I made my right angled turn stubbed my toe on the platform and probably shook Her Majesty a bit. 'You've done it again,' I remember chiding myself. But I'm sure the Queen was well used to people being nervous. I had often walked out and played in front of 100,000 crowds and more, yet this was a very different kind of excitement.

I bowed and she shook my hand before placing the medal in a clip which had been put on my jacket. This was yet another example of the fine detail and painstaking planning which goes into these occasions. No chance of embarrassed fumbling or being stabbed by a sharp needle!

Before the investiture it had been hinted that the Queen might not be there and that a representative could carry out the presentations so I was glad of the chance to meet her after all – even though I was nervous. She spoke well about football and when I explained to her that I had retired from playing but was coaching the younger players she said, 'It must be very rewarding after being involved as a player so long yourself.' I was really surprised at how much she knew about my background with Celtic and, realizing I was getting into a bit of a conversation, tried very hard to slow down my rather fast speech. I became aware that she was spending a lot more time with me than many of the others, it must have been a good few minutes because Kathryn and the children mentioned it later. Again the Queen offered a handshake and I took my leave feeling a sense of pride as I saw my family sitting there. Kathryn admitted to a wee lump in her throat and a tear in her eye.

As we left, the band again struck up 'God Save the Queen' and I wondered if the poor lady ever got fed up with listening to it!

Everyone has their own views on royalty, politics, religion and many other aspects of life. From the experience I had at Holyrood I would say this: I found the Queen to be a lovely lady. What I remember vividly about her is that she had a marvellously fine skin and she looked a lot younger in person than she does on television or in newspaper photographs. I was really impressed and I think it will be a while yet before Prince Charles is king!

Afterwards we went out into the gardens where we were reunited with two proud grannies and Jeff, and it was at this point that I had probably my most uneasy moment of the day.

As I walked out of the palace door there must have been about fifteen press photographers all waiting for *me*. I was getting the real superstar treatment as they asked me to pose for this picture and that one and could we just do another one here, Bobby. It was the usual press situation. At one stage I glanced to the side and saw I was getting some attention from a queue of people beside a sign which proclaimed: Official photographs. There in the queue were new Knights of the Realm, the odd Companion of the Bath and probably a few millionaires amongst them. And here was wee Bobby Lennox, MBE, getting the treatment. It brought home once again just what a football-mad country this really is.

When that ordeal was over we went to a nearby hotel, had a nice meal and then set out for Saltcoats.

The minute I got into the house, the top hat and tails were exchanged for the old denims and training shoes.

I put my feet up, opened a can of lager and watched the telly.

It was the perfect end to a marvellous and proud day for the Lennox family.

# 12

# I Become a Coach

As a football player you have a responsibility mainly for yourself through your fitness and attitude, although it's also important to realize you are part of a team set-up. As a player you tend to follow instructions – to do exactly what you are told. That doesn't mean to say that all players are blinkered or stupid and can't think for themselves.

I'm making these points to show what a change I experienced from being a player one day and a coach just twenty-four hours later. It's a daunting task suddenly facing, say, thirty players when you're thinking, is this the right thing to be doing or saying? Am I cut out for this type of job?

Right away I must say how fortunate I was to take over the reserve side with Billy McNeill, John Clark and Jim Lumsden there. Each has been a tower of strength – especially in the early weeks and months. Added to that I got tremendous help from Danny McGrain and Roy Aitken who, at the drop of a hat, would come and help me with the younger players.

A typical training session at Celtic Park starts with all the players together, then after a while we split into first and second team squads. Danny and Roy are always the front runners, leading by example and the minute they see any routine in which I need help they give it. Jim Lumsden, in charge of the youth team, has a lot of experience in dealing with players, so in the early days I followed his advice closely when it came to mapping out training routines.

When Billy or John are busy I help out with the first team. Again I've had nothing but the utmost cooperation and respect from the players – including those with whom I played for so many years. It is during these training sessions that you appreciate the real professionalism at Celtic Park. There is no pettiness on the training ground. People buckle down and do the job. There are no prima donnas.

I admit that at first I found it difficult to speak to a group of players in the dressing room. When you've been used to being a listener all your life it can be difficult to take charge of a team. The first few times I simply read out the team list and then talked to players individually. To an extent I still prefer it that way. I think you can do more for a player's confidence that way, even if you're talking to him about mistakes.

Yet there are times when a face-to-face is necessary. I told the team once that as a former player myself I found it a bit awkward to talk to them as a group because managers tend to be repetitive. But we had lost two goals in the previous game through elementary mistakes. 'I may repeat myself,' I told them, 'but it's only because you are making the same mistakes week after week and we have to keep talking about them. I'm no longer embarrassed.'

The first few days I felt myself lacking in confidence because coaching was a whole new world to me then. But the same is true for anyone taking on a new job. The one thing that kept me going was the fact that for many years I had trained and learned under the guidance of Jock Stein and I remembered many of his methods. Even during training sessions little things would stir in the back of my mind and to vary the programme I would get the lads to try them out.

As far as dealing with younger players is concerned I'm fortunate that a generation or two has elapsed and I think this makes for a healthier atmosphere.

And talking of atmosphere I got a taste of what it's like at the top when I was called upon to assist Billy McNeill for the very important European Cup first-round second-leg tie between Juventus and Celtic in Italy in season 1981–2.

I had been over the course so many times with Billy as a player in this particular tournament but I was to learn that management at that level is something completely different. I remember walking out behind the players onto the Stadio Comunale and hearing the familiar bedlam from a 70,000 crowd. But when the players crossed the dividing white line and we turned left to the dugout my stomach was knotted. Suddenly there was nothing more we could do – they were on their own with only a slender one-goal lead. I think I can understand now why managers have ulcers and take valium tablets. At least on the field you can get involved and change the course of a match. In the dugout you can only feel a sense of sheer frustration when things are going wrong. Out on the field if people are having a kick at you as often as not you don't even notice. But from the dugout you see every shady tactic in the book.

Even though we suffered a bitter defeat that night and lost 2–0 it gave me cause to hope that some day I could go on to be a manager at that level. I know I've always been a great one for saying that I never look too far ahead but I think that everyone in football who wants to stay with the game wants to be a manager – ulcers and all.

I can also understand even more now the need for a manager to have a good assistant to back him up. You need someone in that capacity – someone to bounce ideas off and someone who can tell you when you're heading off course. Managers are often called to their offices to deal with all the problems which beset any club and there are days when he can't even take part in training because of other commitments. Luckily, looking after youngsters, there isn't much to distract you and I find at present that I'm getting the chance to learn this new part of my trade. It must be very, very difficult to step right into a top managerial post without having served an apprenticeship.

Managing and coaching is extremely time consuming and the higher up the ladder you climb the worse it gets. As a family man I would always have to take into account just how it would affect my home life in the long term. As a player you arrive at the ground, put on your gear, train, have a shower and go home. Management and coaching staff are there before the players in the morning and still there long after they have left. On a typical day I leave Saltcoats at about eight o'clock in the morning and train at Parkhead until around midday. On a Tuesday I help Jim Lumsden with the youth players which means getting home about 9.30 p.m. – so that's a fourteen-hour day. On Wednesdays, if we have no match, we all take in a game with Billy McNeill expecting us to give him an update on how a particular team – often one we're about to meet – are playing and how certain individuals are performing. Overall it's a good thing for the club and everyone works really hard for the common cause.

It's not a hard life, I'm not suggesting that, I know that many people work longer hours for less rewards. And it's great to be in a job where you can keep fit and enjoy a sauna and shower afterwards. But there's no doubt the demands are greater than in my playing days.

The one aspect of my new job that I don't enjoy is that I don't get to see my favourite team – Celtic! Even if we have played our reserve game before a Saturday I know that while I'd love to watch our first team my duty lies elsewhere. Deep down I know my job demands that I help plan for future games and Jim Lumsden and our scout John Kelman do likewise.

The only first team games I've seen I could count on the fingers of one hand and that's a bit annoying when I go down to my pub and have a chat and a pint with the customers. When they start arguing about Celtic I'm at a disadvantage because they've been at the game and I've been elsewhere. Thank goodness at least that this is the age of the video!

Well, that more or less brings the Bobby Lennox story up to date although I hope there will be more chapters in the years ahead. I've been lucky in life and if the years ahead are half as good as the ones gone by I'll be a happy man.

I have a wonderful and loyal wife, three lovely children and a nice home in my beloved Saltcoats. And after more than twenty years I'm still with the club of my dreams.

Whatever the future holds I will always look back on the two decades of my playing career with deep affection and much gratitude. To everyone who helped me reach the top as a player I give my thanks.

And to the wonderful people who populate the slopes of Paradise and who encouraged and inspired me over those years – they can never know the debt I owe to them.

# The Lennox Scoring Record

| | L. | L.C. | S.C. | G.C. | E.C. | D.C. |
|---|---|---|---|---|---|---|
| 1963–4 | 1 | 0 | 0 | 0 | 1 | 0 |
| 1964–5 | 9 | 1 | 6 | 3 | 0 | 0 |
| 1965–6 | 15 | 5 | 1 | 0 | 4 | 0 |
| 1966–7 | 13 | 5 | 5 | 7 | 2 | 0 |
| 1967–8 | 32 | 7 | 0 | 3 | 2 | 0 |
| 1968–9 | 12 | 14 | 3 | 0 | 1 | 0 |
| 1969–70 | 14 | 2 | 3 | 0 | 0 | 0 |
| 1970–1 | 10 | 6 | 4 | 0 | 1 | 0 |
| 1971–2 | 12 | 4 | 2 | 0 | 1 | 0 |
| 1972–3 | 11 | 5 | 1 | 0 | 0 | 0 |
| 1973–4 | 12 | 6 | 2 | 0 | 1 | 5 |
| 1974–5 | 5 | 2 | 0 | 0 | 0 | 1 |
| 1975–6 | 10 | 3 | 0 | 0 | 0 | 0 |
| 1976–7 | 2 | 0 | 0 | 0 | 0 | 0 |
| 1977–8 | 0 | 0 | 0 | 0 | 1 | 0 |
| 1978–9 | 4 | 1 | 1 | 0 | 0 | 0 |
| 1979–80 | 6 | 1 | 3 | 1 | 0 | 2 |
| | 168 | 62 | 31 | 14 | 14 | 8 |

| | |
|---|---|
| League championship | 168 |
| League Cup | 62 |
| Scottish Cup | 31 |
| Glasgow Cup | 14 |
| European Cup and Cup Winners' Cup | 14 |
| Drybrough Cup | 8 |
| | 297 |

Bobby Lennox took his scoring record over the 300 mark with memorable goals in major challenge and testimonial matches against top class opposition.

7 Aug. 1965: v Sunderland at Roker Park. Sunderland 0, Celtic 5. (Lennox one goal)

21 May 1966: v Tottenham Hotspur at Varsity Stadium, Toronto. Celtic 1, Spurs 0. (Lennox one goal)

1 June 1966: v Tottenham Hotspur at Kezar Stadium, San Francisco. Celtic 2, Spurs 1. (Lennox one goal)

5 June 1966: v Tottenham Hotspur at Empire Stadium, Vancouver. Celtic 1, Spurs 1. (Lennox one goal.) Completing unusual feat of scoring in all three games against Spurs in North American tour.

9 June 1966: v Bayern Munich at Kezar Stadium, San Francisco. Celtic 2, Bayern 2. (Lennox one goal)

Lennox scored 19 of Celtic's 47 goals in their unbeaten eleven-game tour of Bermuda, USA and Canada (won 8, drew 3, lost only 6 goals). Bayern Munich were West German Cup Winners and in May 1967 won the European Cup Winners' Cup. Tottenham won the FA Cup in May 1967.

6 Aug. 1966: v Manchester United at Celtic Park. Celtic 4, Manchester United 1. (Lennox one goal)

7 June 1967: v Real Madrid at Santiago Bernabeu Stadium, Madrid. Real Madrid 0, Celtic 1. (Lennox one goal)

8 March 1968: v Newcastle at Celtic Park. Celtic 2, Newcastle United 3. (Lennox one goal)

A.C. Milan were Italian champions and European Cup Winners' Cup holders. The following season they won the European Cup.

1 June 1968: v A.C. Milan at C.N.E. Stadium, Toronto. Celtic 2, A.C. Milan 0. (Lennox one goal.) Celtic won the Canadian National Exhibition Cup of Champions with this victory. The match was watched by 30,000 spectators – the largest soccer crowd in Canada to that date.

30 July 1969: v St. Etienne at Stade Geoffroy Guichard, St. Etienne. St. Etienne 1, Celtic 1. (Lennox one goal)

5 Aug. 1969: v Leeds United at Celtic Park. Celtic 1, Leeds United 1. (Lennox one goal)

22 May 1970: v Eintracht Frankfurt at Downing Stadium, Randall's Island, New York. Celtic 1, Eintracht 3. (Lennox one goal)

16 Nov. 1970: v West Ham Utd at Upton Park (Bobby Moore Testimonial Match). West Ham 3, Celtic 3. (Lennox one goal)

1 Sept. 1971: v Nacional of Uruguay at Celtic Park. Celtic 3, Nacional 0. (Lennox two goals.) This match marked the official opening by Jimmy McGrory of the new Parkhead stand. Nacional were current South American champions.

7 May 1973: v Leeds Utd at Elland Road (Jackie Charlton Testimonial Match). Leeds Utd 3, Celtic 4. (Lennox one goal)

2 Aug. 1973: v Penarol of Uruguay at Celtic Park. Celtic 3, Penarol 1. (Lennox one goal, pen.)

13 May 1974: v Liverpool at Anfield (Roy Yeats Testimonial Match). Liverpool 1, Celtic 4. (Lennox one goal)

17 May 1976: v Manchester United at Celtic Park (Bobby Lennox/Jimmy Johnstone Testimonial Match). Celtic 4, Manchester Utd 0. (Lennox one goal)

7 Aug. 1976: v Penarol of Uruguay at Celtic Park. Celtic 3, Penarol 0. (Lennox one goal)

17 July 1977: v Red Star Belgrade at National Stadium, Singapore (final of Singapore tournament). Celtic 1, Red Star 3. (Lennox one goal)

As can be seen, all of these matches were against top-rated opposition and were keenly contested. Adding the twenty-one goals in these games to those in European and domestic competitions the Lennox tally is taken to an amazing 318 goals, not counting Reserve football and minor friendlies.

It's a record which puts him second only to the great Jimmy McGrory in Celtic's history and a record which will always guarantee him a special place in the hearts of all Celts.